FTCE Middle Grades English 5-9

Teacher Certification Exam

By: Sharon A. Wynne, M.S.

XAMonline, Inc.

Boston

XAMonline, Inc.
21 Orient Avenue
Melrose, MA 02176
Toll Free 1-800-301-4647
Email: info@xamonline.com
Web www.xamonline.com

Library of Congress Cataloging-in-Publication Data
Wynne, Sharon A.

    FTCE Middle Grades English 5-9: Teacher Certification / Sharon A. Wynne.
    ISBN 978-1-64239-010-0

1. Middle Grades English 5-9   2. Study Guides.   3. FTCE
4. Teachers' Certification & Licensure.   5. Careers

Disclaimer:
The opinions expressed in this publication are the sole works of XAMonline and were created independently from the National Education Association, Educational Testing Service, or any State Department of Education, National Evaluation Systems or other testing affiliates.

Between the time of publication and printing, state specific standards as well as testing formats and website information may change that is not included in part or in whole within this product. XAMonline developed the sample test questions and the questions reflect similar content as on real tests; however, they are not former tests. XAMonline assembles content that aligns with state standards but makes no claims nor guarantees teacher candidates a passing score. Numerical scores are determined by testing companies such as NES or ETS and then are compared with individual state standards. A passing score varies from state to state.

Printed in the United States of America

FTCE: Middle Grades English 5-9
ISBN: 978-1-64239-010-0

Table of Contents

Great Study and Testing Tips!

What to study in order to prepare for the subject assessments is the focus of this study guide but equally important is *how* you study.

You can increase your chances of truly mastering the information by taking some simple, but effective steps.

Study Tips:

1. Some foods aid the learning process. Foods such as milk, nuts, seeds, rice, and oats help your study efforts by releasing natural memory enhancers called CCKs (*cholecystokinin*) composed of *tryptophan*, *choline*, and *phenylalanine*. All of these chemicals enhance the neurotransmitters associated with memory. Before studying, try a light, protein-rich meal of eggs, turkey, and fish. All of these foods release the memory enhancing chemicals. The better the connections, the more you comprehend.

Likewise, before you take a test, stick to a light snack of energy boosting and relaxing foods. A glass of milk, a piece of fruit, or some peanuts all release various memory-boosting chemicals and help you to relax and focus on the subject at hand.

2. Learn to take great notes. A by-product of our modern culture is that we have grown accustomed to getting our information in short doses (i.e. TV news sound bites or USA Today style newspaper articles.)

Consequently, we've subconsciously trained ourselves to assimilate information better in neat little packages. If your notes are scrawled all over the paper, it fragments the flow of the information. Strive for clarity. Newspapers use a standard format to achieve clarity. Your notes can be much clearer through use of proper formatting. A very effective format is called the *"Cornell Method."*

> Take a sheet of loose-leaf lined notebook paper and draw a line all the way down the paper about 1-2" from the left-hand edge.

> Draw another line across the width of the paper about 1-2" up from the bottom. Repeat this process on the reverse side of the page.

Look at the highly effective result. You have ample room for notes, a left hand margin for special emphasis items or inserting supplementary data from the textbook, a large area at the bottom for a brief summary, and a little rectangular space for just about anything you want.

3. Get the concept then the details. Too often we focus on the details and don't gather an understanding of the concept. However, if you simply memorize only dates, places, or names, you may well miss the whole point of the subject.

A key way to understand things is to put them in your own words. If you are working from a textbook, automatically summarize each paragraph in your mind. If you are outlining text, don't simply copy the author's words.

Rephrase them in your own words. You remember your own thoughts and words much better than someone else's, and subconsciously tend to associate the important details to the core concepts.

4. Ask Why? Pull apart written material paragraph by paragraph and don't forget the captions under the illustrations.

Example: If the heading is "Stream Erosion", flip it around to read "Why do streams erode?" Then answer the questions.

If you train your mind to think in a series of questions and answers, not only will you learn more, but it also helps to lessen the test anxiety because you are used to answering questions.

5. Read for reinforcement and future needs. Even if you only have 10 minutes, put your notes or a book in your hand. Your mind is similar to a computer; you have to input data in order to have it processed. *By reading, you are creating the neural connections for future retrieval.* The more times you read something, the more you reinforce the learning of ideas.

Even if you don't fully understand something on the first pass, *your mind stores much of the material for later recall.*

6. Relax to learn so go into exile. Our bodies respond to an inner clock called biorhythms. Burning the midnight oil works well for some people, but not everyone.

If possible, set aside a particular place to study that is free of distractions. Shut off the television, cell phone, and pager and exile your friends and family during your study period.

If you really are bothered by silence, try background music. Light classical music at a low volume has been shown to aid in concentration over other types. Music that evokes pleasant emotions without lyrics is highly suggested. Try just about anything by Mozart. It relaxes you.

7. <u>**Use arrows not highlighters**</u>. At best, it's difficult to read a page full of yellow, pink, blue, and green streaks. Try staring at a neon sign for a while and you'll soon see that the horde of colors obscure the message.

A quick note, a brief dash of color, an underline, and an arrow pointing to a particular passage is much clearer than a horde of highlighted words.

8. <u>**Budget your study time**</u>. Although you shouldn't ignore any of the material, *allocate your available study time in the same ratio that topics may appear on the test.*

Testing Tips:

1. **Get smart, play dumb. Don't read anything into the question.** Don't make an assumption that the test writer is looking for something else than what is asked. Stick to the question as written and don't read extra things into it.

2. **Read the question and all the choices *twice* before answering the question.** You may miss something by not carefully reading, and then re-reading both the question and the answers.

If you really don't have a clue as to the right answer, leave it blank on the first time through. Go on to the other questions, as they may provide a clue as to how to answer the skipped questions.

If later on, you still can't answer the skipped ones . . . *Guess.* The only penalty for guessing is that you *might* get it wrong. Only one thing is certain; if you don't put anything down, you will get it wrong!

3. **Turn the question into a statement.** Look at the way the questions are worded. The syntax of the question usually provides a clue. Does it seem more familiar as a statement rather than as a question? Does it sound strange?

By turning a question into a statement, you may be able to spot if an answer sounds right, and it may also trigger memories of material you have read.

4. **Look for hidden clues.** It's actually very difficult to compose multiple-foil (choice) questions without giving away part of the answer in the options presented.

In most multiple-choice questions you can often readily eliminate one or two of the potential answers. This leaves you with only two real possibilities and automatically your odds go to Fifty-Fifty for very little work.

5. **Trust your instincts.** For every fact that you have read, you subconsciously retain something of that knowledge. On questions that you aren't really certain about, go with your basic instincts. **Your first impression on how to answer a question is usually correct.**

6. **Mark your answers directly on the test booklet.** Don't bother trying to fill in the optical scan sheet on the first pass through the test.

Just be very careful not to miss-mark your answers when you eventually transcribe them to the scan sheet.

7. **Watch the clock!** You have a set amount of time to answer the questions. Don't get bogged down trying to answer a single question at the expense of 10 questions you can more readily answer.

COMPETENCY 1.0 KNOWLEDGE OF THE CHARACTERISTICS OF MIDDLE GRADES STUDENTS AS RELATED TO THE TEACHING AND LEARNING OF INTEGRATED LANGUAGE ARTS

Skill 1.1 Identify the characteristics of cognitive development of middle grades students as they relate to the teaching of integrated language arts.

The late nineteenth and early twentieth centuries' studies by behaviorists and developmental psychologists significantly affected the manner in which the education community and parents approached the selection of literature for children.

The cognitive development studies of Piaget, the epigenetic view of personality development by Erik Erikson, the formulation of Abraham Maslow's hierarchy of basic needs, and the social learning theory of behaviorists like Alfred Bandura contributed to a greater understanding of child/adolescent development even as these theorists contradicted each other's findings. Though few educators today totally subscribe to Piaget's inflexible stages of mental development, his principles of both qualitative and quantitative mental capacity, his generalizations about the parallels between physical growth and thinking capacity, and his support of the adolescent's heightened moral perspective are still used as measures by which to evaluate child/adolescent literature.

Piaget's four stages of mental development:

- Sensimotor intelligence (birth to age two) deals with the pre-language period of development. The child is most concerned with coordinating movement and action. Words begin to represent people and things.

- Preoperational thought is the period spanning ages 2-12. It is broken into several substages.

    1. Preconceptual (2-4) phase—most behavior is based on subjective judgment.

    2. Intuitive (4-7) phase—children use language to verbalize their experiences and mental processes.

- Concrete operations (7-11)—children begin to apply logic to concrete objects and experiences. They can combine performance and reasoning to solve problems.

- Formal operations (12-15)—adolescents begin to think beyond the immediate and to theorize. They apply formal logic to interpreting abstract constructions and to recognizing experiences that are contrary to fact.

Though Piaget presented these stages as progressing sequentially, a given child might enter any period earlier or later than most children. Furthermore, a child might perform at different levels in different situations. Thus, a fourteen-year-old female might be able to function at the formal operations stage in a literature class but function at a concrete operations level in mathematical concepts.

Piaget's Theories Influence Literature

Most middle school students have reached the concrete-operations level. By this time they have left behind their egocentrism and are experiencing a need to understand the physical and social world around them. They become more interested in ways to relate to other people. Their favorite stories become those about real people rather than animals or fairy-tale characters. The conflicts in their literature are internal as well as external. Books like Paula Fox's *The Stone-Faced Boy*, Betsy Byards' *The Midnight Fox*, and Lois Lenski's *Strawberry Girl* deal with a child's loneliness, confusion about identity or loyalty, and poverty. Pre-adolescents are becoming more cognizant of and interested in the past, resulting in a love of adventure stories about national heroes like Davy Crockett, Daniel Boone, and Abe Lincoln and biographies/autobiographies of real-life heroes, like Jackie Robinson and Cesar Chavez. At this level, children also become interested in the future, thus their love of both fantasy (most medieval in spirit) and science fiction.

The seven-to-eleven year olds also internalize moral values. They are concerned with their sense of self and are willing to question rules and adult authority. In books such as Beverly Cleary's *Henry Huggins* and *Mitch and Amy*, the protagonists are children pursuing their own desires with the same frustrations as other children. When these books were written in the 1960s, returning a found pet or overcoming a reading disability were common problems.

From twelve to fifteen, adolescents advance beyond the concrete-operations level to begin developing communication skills that enable them to articulate attitudes/opinions and exchange knowledge. They can distinguish , and contrast, historical fiction from pure history and biography. They can identify the elements of literature and their relationships within a specific story. As their thinking becomes more complex, early adolescents become increasingly sensitive to others' emotions and reactions. They become better able to suspend their disbelief and enter the world of literature, thus expanding their perceptions of the real world.

In discussing the adolescent's moral judgment, Piaget noted that after age eleven, children stopped viewing actions as either "right" or "wrong." The older child considers both the intent and the behavior in its context. A younger child would view an accidental destruction of property in terms of the amount of damage The older child, by contrast, rises to a contextual and moral view, forgiving accidental damage, even when it is greater in degree, and condemning loss brought about by deliberate malice.

Kohlberg's Theories of Moral Development

Expanding on Piaget's thinking, Lawrence Kohlberg developed a hierarchy of values. Though progressive, the stages of Kohlberg's hierarchy are not clearly aligned to chronological age. The six stages of development correlate to three levels of moral judgment.

Level I. Moral values reside in external acts rather than in persons or standards.

Stage 0. Premoral. No association of actions or needs with sense of right or wrong.

Stage 1. Obedience and punishment orientation. Child defers to adult authority. His actions are motivated by a desire to stay out of trouble.

Stage 2. Right action/self-interest orientation. Performance of right deeds results in needing satisfaction.

Level II. Moral values reside in maintaining conventions of right behavior.

Stage 3. Good-person orientation. The child performs right actions to receive approval from others, conforming to the same standards.

Stage 4. Law-and-order orientation. Doing one's duty and showing respect for authority contributes to maintaining social order.

Level III. Moral values reside in principles separate in association from the persons or agencies that enforce these principles.

Stage 5. Prior-rights-and-social-contract orientation. The rules of society are accepted as correct but alterable. Privileges and duties are derived from social contact. Obedience to society's rules protects the rights of self and others.

Stage 6. Conscience orientation. Ethical standards, such as justice, equality, and respect for others, guide moral conduct more than legal rules.

Though these stages represent a natural progression of values-to-actions relationships, persons may regress to an earlier stage in certain situations. An adolescent already operating at Stage 5 may regress to Stage 3 in a classroom where consequences of non-conformity are met with disapproval or punishment.

An adult operating at Stage 6 may regress to Stage 4 when obligated by military training or confronted with a conflict between self-preservation and the protection of others.

Values clarification education based on Piaget's and Kohlberg's theories imply that development is inherent in human socialization. Becoming a decent person is a natural result of human development.

Social Learning Theory

Much of traditional learning theory resulted from the work of early behaviorists like B. F. Skinner and has been refined by modern theorists such as Albert Bandura. Behaviorists believe that intellectual, and therefore behavioral, development cannot be divided into specific stages. They believe that behavior is the result of conditioning experiences, a continuum of rewards and punishments. Environmental conditions are viewed as greater stimuli than inherent qualities. Thus in social-learning theory the consequences of behavior—that is, the rewards or punishments—are more significant in social development than are the motivations for the behavior.

Bandura also proposed that a child learns vicariously through observing the behavior of others whereas the developmental psychologists presumed that children developed through the actual self-experience.

The Humanistic Theory of Development

No discussion of child development would be complete without a review of Abraham Maslow's hierarchy of needs, from basic physiological needs to the need for self-actualization. The following list represents those needs from the hierarchy that most affect children.

1. **Need for physical well-being**. In young children the provisions for shelter, food, clothing, and protection by significant adults satisfy this need. In older children, this satisfaction of physical comforts translates to a need for material security and may manifest itself in struggles to overcome poverty and maintain the integrity of home and family.

2. **Need for love**. The presumption is that every human being needs to love and be loved. With young children this reciprocal need is directed at and received from parents and other family members, pets, and friends. In older children and adolescents this need for love forms the basis for romance and peer acceptance.

3. **Need to belong**. Beyond the need for one-on-one relationships, a child needs the security of being an accepted member of a group. Young children identify with family, friends, and schoolmates.

   They are concerned with having happy experiences and being accepted by people they love and respect. Later, they associate with community, country, and perhaps world groups. Adolescents become more aware of a larger world order and thus develop concerns about issues facing society, such as political or social unrest, wars, discrimination, and environmental issues. They seek to establish themselves with groups who accept and share their values. They become more team oriented.

4. **Need to achieve competence**. A human's need to interact satisfactorily with his environment begins with the infant's exploration of his immediate surroundings. Visual and tactile identification of objects and persons provides confidence to perform further explorations. To become well adjusted, the child must achieve competence to feel satisfaction. Physical and intellectual achievements become measures of acceptance. Frustrations resulting from physical or mental handicaps are viewed as hurdles to be overcome if satisfaction is to be achieved. Older children view the courage to overcome obstacles as part of the maturing process.

5. **Need to know**. Curiosity is the basis of intelligence. The need to learn is persistent. To maintain intellectual security, children must be able to find answers to their questions in order to stimulate further exploration of information to satisfy that persistent curiosity.

6. **Need for beauty and order**. Aesthetic satisfaction is as important as the need for factual information. Intellectual stimulation comes from satisfying curiosity about the fine as well as the practical arts. Acceptance for one's accomplishments in dance, music, drawing, writing, or performing/ appreciating any of the arts leads to a sense of accomplishment and self-actualization.

Theory of Psychosocial Development

Erik Erikson, a follower of Sigmund Freud, presented the theory that human development consists of maturation through a series of psychosocial crises. The struggle to resolve these crises helps a person achieve individuality as he learns to function in society.

Maturation occurs as the individual moves through a progression of increasingly complex stages. The movement from one stage to the next hinges on the successful resolution of the conflicts encountered in each stage, and each of the stages represents a step in identity formation.

Stage 1 (trust versus distrust), stage 2 (achieving autonomy), and stage 3 (developing initiative) relate to infants and young/middle children. Stages 4 and 5 relate to late childhood through adolescents.

Stage 4 - **Becoming Industrious**. Late childhood, according to Erikson, occurs between seven and eleven. Having already mastered conflicts that helped them to overcome mistrust of unfamiliar persons, places, and things; made them more independent in caring for themselves and their possessions; and overcame their sense of guilt at behavior that creates opposition with others, children are ready to assert themselves in surmounting feelings of inferiority. Children at this stage learn to master independent tasks as well as to work cooperatively with other children. They increasingly measure their own competence by comparing themselves to their peers.

Stage 5 - **Establishing Identity**. From age eleven through the teen years, a person's conflicts arise from his search for identity as an individual and a member of society. Because internal demands for independence and peer acceptance sometimes oppose external demands for conformity to rules and standards, friction with family, school, and society in general occur during these years. The adolescent must resolve issues such as the amount of control he will concede to family and other rule-enforcing adults as he searches for other acceptance models. In his quest for self-identity, he experiments with adult behavior and attitudes. At the end of his teen years, he should have a well-established sense of identity.

Theory of multiple intelligences

Howard Gardner's research in the 1980s has been recently influential in helping teachers understand that human beings process information differently and, therefore, communicate their knowledge through different modes of operation. It is important to present language and literature in visual, auditory, tactile, and kinesthetic ways to allow every child to develop good skills through his own mode of learning. Then the child himself must be allowed to perform through the strength of his intelligence. The movement toward learning academies in the practical and fine arts and in the sciences is a result of our growing understanding of all aspects of child development.

Modern society's role in child development

Despite their differences, there are many similarities in the theories of child development. However, most of these theories were developed prior to the social unrest of the 1970s. In industrialized western society, children are increasingly excluded from the activities of work and play with adults, and education has become their main occupation. This exclusion tends to prolong childhood and adolescence and thus inhibit development as visualized by theorists.
For adolescents in America, this prolonging results in slower social and intellectual maturation contrasted with increasing physical maturity. Adolescents today deal with drugs, violence, communicable diseases, and a host of social problems that were of minimal concern thirty years ago. Even pre-adolescent children are dealing with poverty, disease, broken homes, abuse, and drugs.

Influence of Theories on Literature

All of these development theories and existing social conditions influence the literature created and selected for and by child/adolescent readers.

Child/adolescent literature has always been to some degree didactic, whether non-fiction or fiction. Until the twentieth century, "kiddie lit" was also morally prescriptive. Written by adults who determined either what they believed children needed or liked or what they should need or like, most books, stories, poems, and essays dealt with experiences or issues that would make children into better adults. The fables, fairy tales, and epics set the moral/social standards of their times while entertaining the child in every reader/listener. These tales are still popular because they have a universal appeal. Except for the rare exceptions discussed earlier in this section, most books were written for literate adults. Educated children found their pleasure in the literature that was available.

Benefits of research

One benefit of the child-development and learning-theory research is that they provide guidelines for writers, publishers, and educators to follow in the creation, marketing, and selection of good reading materials. MacMillan introduced children's literature as a separate publishing market in 1918. By the 1930s, most major publishers had a children's department. Though arguments have existed throughout this century about quality versus quantity, there is no doubt that children's literature is a significant slice of the market pie.

Another influence is that children's books are a reflection of both developmental theories and social changes. Reading provides children with the opportunity to become more aware of societal differences, to measure their behavior against the behavior of realistic fictional characters or the subjects of biographies, to become informed about events of the past and present that will affect their futures, and to acquire a genuine appreciation of literature.

Furthermore, there is an obligation for adults to provide instruction and entertainment that all children in our democratic society can use. As parents and educators we have a further obligation to guide children in the selection of books that are appropriate to their reading ability and interest levels. Of course, there is a fine line between guidance and censorship. As with discipline, parents learn that to make forbidden is to make more desirable. To publish a list of banned books is to make them suddenly attractive.

Most children/adolescents left to their own selections will choose books on topics that interest them and are written in language they can understand.

Skill 1.2   Identify the characteristics of social and emotional development of middle grades students as they relate to the teaching of integrated language arts.

Adolescent literature, because of the age range of readers, is extremely diverse. Fiction for the middle group, usually ages ten/eleven to fourteen/fifteen, deals with issues of coping with internal and external changes in their lives. Because children's writers in the twentieth century have produced increasingly realistic fiction, adolescents can now find problems dealt with honestly in novels.

Teachers of middle/junior high school students see the greatest change in interests and reading abilities. Fifth and sixth graders, included in elementary grades in many schools, are viewed as older children while seventh and eighth graders are preadolescent. Ninth graders, included sometimes as top dogs in junior high school and sometimes as underlings in high school, definitely view themselves as teenagers. Their literature choices will often be governed more by interest than by ability, thus the wealth of high-interest, low-readability books that have flooded the market in recent years. Tenth through twelfth graders will still select high-interest books for pleasure reading but are also easily encouraged to stretch their literature muscles by reading more classics.

Because of the rapid social changes, topics that once did not interest young people until they reached their teens—suicide, gangs, homosexuality—are now subjects of books for even younger readers. The plethora of high-interest books reveals how desperately schools have failed to produce on-level readers and how the market has adapted to that need. However, these high-interest books are now readable for younger children whose reading levels are at or above normal. No matter how tastefully written, some contents are inappropriate for younger readers. The problem becomes not so much steering them toward books that they have the reading ability to handle, but encouraging them toward books whose content is appropriate to their levels of cognitive and social development. A fifth-grader may be able to read V.C. Andrews' *Flowers in the Attic* but not possess the social/moral development to handle the deviant behavior of the characters. At the same time, because of the complex changes affecting adolescents, the teacher must be well versed in learning theory and child development as well as competent to teach the subject matter of language and literature.

COMPETENCY 2.0 KNOWLEDGE OF RESEARCH AND CURRENT ISSUES IN TEACHING INTEGRATED LANGUAGE ARTS

Skill 2.1   Identify current issues in middle grades language arts curricula.

Learning approach

Early theories of language development were formulated from learning theory research. The assumption was that language development evolved from learning the rules of language structures and applying them through imitation and reinforcement. This approach also assumed that linguistic, cognitive, and social developments were independent of each other. Thus, children were expected to learn language from patterning after adults who spoke and wrote Standard English. No allowance was made for communication through child jargon, idiomatic expressions, or grammatical and mechanical errors resulting from too strict adherence to the rules of inflection (*childs* instead of *children*) or conjugation (*runned* instead of *ran*). No association was made between physical and operational development and language mastery.

Linguistic approach

Studies spearheaded by Noam Chomsky in the 1950s formulated the theory that language ability is innate and develops through natural human maturation as environmental stimuli trigger acquisition of syntactical structures appropriate to each exposure level. The assumption of a hierarchy of syntax downplayed the significance of semantics. Because of the complexity of syntax and the relative speed with which children acquire language, linguists attributed language development to biological rather than cognitive or social influences.

Cognitive approach

Researchers in the 1970s proposed that language knowledge derives from both syntactic and semantic structures. Drawing on the studies of Piaget and other cognitive learning theorists (see Skill 1.1), supporters of the cognitive approach maintained that children acquire knowledge of linguistic structures after they have acquired the cognitive structures necessary to process language. For example, joining words for specific meaning necessitates sensory motor intelligence. The child must be able to coordinate movement and recognize objects before she can identify words to name the objects or word groups to describe the actions performed with those objects.

Adolescents must have developed the mental abilities for *organizing concepts as well as concrete operations*, *predicting outcomes*, and *theorizing* before they can assimilate and verbalize complex sentence structures, choose vocabulary for particular nuances of meaning, and examine semantic structures for tone and manipulative effect.

Sociocognitive approach

Other theorists in the 1970s proposed that language development results from sociolinguistic competence. Language, cognitive, and social knowledge are interactive elements of total human development. Emphasis on verbal communication as the medium for language expression resulted in the inclusion of speech activities in most language-arts curricula.

Unlike previous approaches, the sociocognitive approach allowed that determining the appropriateness of language in given situations for specific listeners is as important as understanding semantic and syntactic structures. By engaging in conversation, children at all stages of development have opportunities to test their language skills, receive feedback, and make modifications. As a social activity, conversation is as structured by social order as grammar is structured by the rules of syntax. Conversation satisfies the learner's need to be heard and understood and to influence others. Thus, his choices of vocabulary, tone, and content are dictated by his ability to assess the language knowledge of his listeners. He is constantly applying his cognitive skills to using language in a social interaction. If the capacity to acquire language is inborn, without an environment in which to practice language, a child would not pass beyond grunts and gestures as did primitive man.

Of course, the varying degrees of environmental stimuli to which children are exposed at all age levels creates a slower or faster development of language. Some children are prepared to articulate concepts and recognize symbolism by the time they enter fifth grade. They have been exposed to challenging reading and conversations with well-spoken adults at home or in their social groups. Others are still trying to master sight-recognition skills and are not yet ready to combine words in complex patterns.

Concerns for the teacher

Because teachers must, by virtue of tradition and the dictates of the curriculum, teach grammar, usage, and writing as well as reading and later literature, the problem becomes when to teach what to whom. The profusion of approaches to teaching grammar alone are mind-boggling. In the universities, we learn about transformational grammar, stratificational grammar, sectoral grammar, etc.

But in practice, most teachers, supported by presentations in textbooks and by the methods they learned themselves, keep coming back to the same traditional prescriptive approach—read and imitate—or structural approach—learn the parts of speech, the parts of the sentence, punctuation rules, sentence patterns. After enough of the terminology and rules are stored in the brain, then we learn to write and speak. For some educators, the best solution is the worst—don't teach grammar at all.

The same problems occur in teaching usage. How much can we demand that students communicate in Standard English only? Different schools of thought suggest that a study of dialect and idiom and recognition of various jargons is a vital part of language development. Social pressures, especially on students in middle and junior high schools, to be accepted within their peer groups and to speak the non-standard language spoken outside the school make adolescents resistant to the corrective, remedial approach. In many communities where the immigrant populations are high, new words are entering English from other languages even as words and expressions that were common when we were children have become rare or obsolete.

Regardless of differences of opinion concerning language development, it is safe to say that a language arts teacher will be most effective using the styles and approaches with which she is most comfortable. And, if she subscribes to a student-centered approach, she may find that the students have a lot to teach her and each other. Moffett and Wagner in the Fourth Edition of *Student-Centered Language Arts K-12* stress the three I's: individualization, interaction, and integration. Essentially, they are supporting the socio-cognitive approach to language development. By providing an opportunity for the student to select his own activities and resources, his instruction is individualized. By centering on and teaching each other, students are interactive. Finally, by allowing students to synthesize a variety of knowledge structures, they integrate them. The teacher's role becomes that of a facilitator.

Benefits of the socio-cognitive approach

This approach has tended to guide the whole language movement, currently in fashion. Most basal readers utilize an integrated, cross-curricular approach to successful grammar, language, and usage. Reinforcement becomes an intradepartmental responsibility. Language incorporates diction and terminology across the curriculum. Standard usage is encouraged and supported by both the core classroom textbooks and current software for technology. Teachers need to acquaint themselves with the computer capabilities in their school district and at their individual school sites. Advances in new technologies require the teacher to familiarize herself with programs that would serve her students' needs. Students respond enthusiastically to technology. Several highly effective programs are available in various formats to assist students with initial instruction or remediation.

Grammar texts such as the Warriner series employ various methods to reach individual learning styles. The school library media center should become a focal point for individual exploration.

Skill 2.2   Identify research related to the teaching of integrated language arts.

Need for Research. Many more teachers today are trying to integrate reading and writing into their curriculum in the belief that such integration of language arts and other subjects will help their students learn more. They are responding, in part, to national calls for students who are able to read, write, and think critically. They are also responding to the need for some efficiency in presenting an ever-expanding curriculum. However, simply mixing subjects may not help students either learn basic facts or develop higher thinking and literacy skills. In a recent national survey, teachers and state language arts specialists identified the need to know more about whether and how to integrate the elementary curriculum as their top concern overall.

What are the characteristics of and outcomes produced by effective integrated elementary language arts instruction? A set of contrasting case studies has examined pairs of grade 1 and grade 4 classrooms in six states to identify the characteristics of effective literacy instruction. In addition to classroom observations of student engagement, student achievement has been assessed through reading and writing samples and standardized tests such as McGraw Hill's *Terra Nova.*

What instructional activities support the development of literacy and the learning of literature and social studies? A five-year longitudinal study in ten classrooms in grades 1-5 in two states involved collaborating with teachers to develop curriculum that integrates literature and social studies. Half of the classrooms were multi-grade (3/4 and 4/5) and half served a single grade (1, 2, 4). All units were designed to meet school and district goals regarding student achievement in literacy skills and in understanding key social studies concepts and literary genres, and then assessed changes in student achievement based on the changes in curriculum. Data included intensive classroom observations, student case studies, standardized test scores, textbook exams, teacher- and researcher-developed performance measures, portfolios, and student and teacher self-assessments.

Educational Significance of the Research. Integrated curriculum is adopted by an increasing number of teachers and schools, it is essential to obtain data about its overall effectiveness as well as the particulars that can make it most effective in enhancing achievement among a diverse population of students.

Research Reports:

- "What Do We Know about Effective Fourth-Grade Teachers and Their Classrooms?" Source: Roller, C. (Ed.). *Learning to Teach Reading: Setting the Research Agenda.* (2001). Newark, DE: International Reading Association.
- "Unpacking Literate Achievement." Source: *Stirring the Waters: A Tribute to Marie Clay.* (1999). Heinemann.

Articles:

- "What Do We Know About Effective Fourth-Grade Teachers and their Classrooms?" (Book Chapter, *Learning to Teach Reading: Setting the Research Agenda*, International Reading Association)
- "Effective Early Literacy Teachers and Student Test Scores." Source: ". Fall 1998.
- "How Do Teachers View and Use New English Language Arts Standards?" Source: *English Update: A Newsletter from the Center on English Learning & Achievement.* Spring 1998.
- "Integrating Curriculum in Elementary Classrooms to Promote High Student Achievement." Source: *English Update: A Newsletter from the Center on English Learning & Achievement.* Spring 1998.

Books:

- *Best Practices in Literacy Instruction* (1999). Linda Gambrell, Lesley Morrow, Susan Neumann, Michael Pressley, Eds.
- *Best Practices in Literacy Instruction*, 2nd edition (2003). Lesley Morrow, Linda Gambrell, Michael Pressley, Eds. The Guilford Press.
- *Reading to Learn: Lessons from Exemplary Fourth-Grade Classrooms* (2002). Richard L. Allington & Peter H. Johnston. The Guilford Press.
- *Reading Instruction That Works: The Case for Balanced Teaching* (1998). Michael Pressley, The Guilford Press.

Skill 2.3   Identify effective interdisciplinary learning experiences within a middle grades classroom.

Any or all of the activities listed below can and should be used to promote creative literary response and analysis:

- Have students take a particular passage from a story and retell it from another character's perspective.
- Challenge students to suggest a sequel or a prequel (what happened before) to any given story they have read.
- Ask the students to recast a story in which the key characters are male into one where the key characters are female (or vice versa). Have them explain how these changes alter the narrative, plot, or outcomes.
- Have the students produce a newspaper as the characters of a given story would have reported the news in their community.

- Transform the story into a ballad poem or a picture book version for younger peers.

An example of an integrated creative writing lesson plan might begin with a discussion about lessons nature can teach us.

- Begin by exploring in a journal a lesson the students have learned from nature. (Writing/pre-reading/prior knowledge)

- Create a brainstorming chart/ cluster on the board from students' responses.
- Students would begin reading selections from NATURE by Ralph Emerson. (Reading)

- Discuss in class the connections. (Speaking/listening)

- Read aloud models of reflective essays on nature's lessons. Next students would go outside and, using a series of guided questions, observe an object in nature. (Writing/viewing)

- Use observations to allow students to write their own reflective essay on an object in nature. (writing) Use of peer response and editing would encourage students to share and improve their writing. (Writing/reading/speaking/listening)

- Read final pieces aloud to the class or publish them on a bulletin board.

Skill 2.4   Identify professional resources for middle grades instructors.

TeachersFirst – The Web Resource for K-12 teachers.
www.teachersfirst.com/matrix.htm

Professional Development in Literacy and Technology Integration.
www.literacy.uconn.edu/prodev.htm
Lists sources for:
- Professional Development in Literacy
- Professional Development in Literacy and Technology Integration
- Training Documents, Learning Modules and Handouts for Professional Development
- Websites Devoted to Staff Development Issues and Resources
- Online Resources to Inspire Discussion within Faculty Study Groups

Skill 2.5 **Identify effective technological resources to use in the integrated middle grades classroom.**

Media's impact on today's society is immense and ever-increasing. As children, we watch programs on television that are amazingly fast-paced and visually rich. Parent's roles as verbal and moral teachers are diminishing in response to the much more stimulating guidance of the television set. Adolescence, which used to be the time for going out and exploring the world first hand, is now consumed by the allure of MTV, popular music, and video games. Young adults are exposed to uncensored sex and violence.

But media's effect on society is beneficial and progressive at the same time. Its effect on education in particular provides special challenges and opportunities for teachers and students.

Thanks to satellite technology, instructional radio and television programs can be received by urban classrooms and rural villages. CD-ROMs can allow students to learn information through a virtual reality experience. The internet allows instant access to unlimited data and connects people across all cultures through shared interests. Educational media, when used in a productive way, enriches instruction and makes it more individualized, accessible, and economical.

COMPETENCY 3.0 KNOWLEDGE OF LITERACY IN THE INTEGRATED LANGUAGE ARTS

Skill 3.1   Identify strategies for developing students' lifelong learning and reading habits.

Reading for enjoyment makes it possible to go to places in the world we will never be able to visit, or perhaps when we learn about the enchantments of a particular place, we will set a goal of going there someday. When *Under the Tuscan Sun* by Frances Mayes was published, it became a best seller. It also increased tourism to Italy. Many of the readers of that book visited Italy for the first time in their lives.

In fiction, we can live through experiences that we will never encounter. We delve into feelings that are similar to our own or are so far removed from our own that we are filled with wonder and curiosity. In fact, we read because we're curious— curious to visit, experience, and know new and different things. The reader lives with a crowd of people and a vast landscape. Life is constantly being enriched by the reading, and the mind is constantly being expanded. To read is to grow. Sometimes the experience of reading a particular book or story is so delicious that we go back and read it again and again, such as the works of Jane Austen. We keep track of what is truly happening in the world when we read current best-sellers because they not only reflect what everyone else is interested in right now, they can influence trends. We can know in-depth what television news cannot cram in by reading publications like *Time* and *Newsweek*.

How do we model this wonderful gift for our students? We can bring those interesting stories into our classrooms and share the excitement we feel when we discover them. We can relate things that make us laugh so students may see the humor and laugh with us. We can vary the established curriculum to include something we are reading that we want to share. The tendency of students nowadays is to receive all of their information from television or the internet. It's important for the teacher to help students understand that television and the internet are not substitutes for reading. They should be an accessory, an extension, a springboard for reading.

Another thing teachers can do to inspire students to become readers is to assign a book that you have never read before and read along with them, chapter by chapter. Run a contest and the winner gets to pick a book that you and they will read chapter by chapter. If you are excited about it and are experiencing satisfaction from the reading, that excitement will be contagious. Be sure that the discussion sessions allow for students to relate what they are thinking and feeling about what they are reading. Lively discussions and the opportunity to express their own feelings will lead to more spontaneous reading.

You can also hand out a reading list of your favorite books and spend some time telling the students what you liked about each. Make sure the list is diverse. It's good to include nonfiction along with fiction. Don't forget that a good biography or autobiography may encourage students to read beyond thrillers and detective stories.

When the class is discussing the latest movie, whether formally as a part of the curriculum or informally and incidentally, if the movie is based on a book, this is a good opportunity to demonstrate how much more can be derived from the reading than from the watching. Or how the two combined make the experience more satisfying and worthwhile.

Share with your students the excitement you have for reading. Successful writers are usually good readers. The two go hand-in-hand.

Skill 3.2 Identify methods for constructing meaning from a variety of reading materials.

1. In order to discover multiple layers of meaning in a **literary work**, the first step is a thorough analysis, examining such things as setting, characters and characterization, plot (focusing particularly on conflicts and pattern of action), theme, tone, figures of speech, and symbolism. It's useful in looking for underlying themes to consider the author's biography, particularly with regard to setting and theme, and the date and time of the writing, paying particular attention to literary undercurrents at the time as well as political and social milieu.

Once the analysis is complete and data accumulated on the historical background, determine the overt meaning. What does the story say about the characters and their conflicts, where does the climax occur, and is there a denouement? Once the forthright, overt meaning is determined, then begin to look for undercurrents, subthemes that are related to the author's life and to what is going on in the literary, political, and social background at the time of writing.

In organization of the presentation, it's usually best to begin with an explication of the overt level of meaning and then follow up with the other messages that emerge from the text.

To *interpret* means essentially to read with understanding and appreciation. It is not as daunting as it is made out to be. Simple techniques for interpreting literature are as follows:

- **Context:** This includes the author's feelings, beliefs, past experiences, goals, needs, and physical environment. Incorporate an understanding of how these elements may have affected the writing to enrich an interpretation of it.

- **Symbols:** Also referred to as a sign, a symbol designates something that stands for something else. In most cases, it is standing for something that has a deeper meaning than its literal denotation. Symbols can have personal, cultural, or universal associations. Use an understanding of symbols to unearth a meaning the author might have intended but not expressed, or even something the author never intended at all.
- **Questions:** Asking questions, such as "How would I react in this situation?" may shed further light on how you feel about the work.

Some important terms for analyzing literature:

Antithesis: Balanced writing about conflicting ideas, usually expressed in sentence form. Some examples are expanding from the center, shedding old habits, and searching never finding.

Aphorism: A focused, succinct expression about life from a sagacious viewpoint. Writings by Ben Franklin, Sir Francis Bacon, and Alexander Pope contain many aphorisms. "Whatever is begun in anger ends in shame" is an aphorism.

Apostrophe: Literary device of addressing an absent or dead person, an abstract idea, or an inanimate object. Sonneteers such as Sir Thomas Wyatt, John Keats, and William Wordsworth, address the moon, stars, and the dead Milton. In William Shakespeare's *Julius Caesar*, Mark Antony addresses the corpse of Caesar in the speech that begins: "O, pardon me, thou bleeding piece of earth, That I am meek and gentle with these butchers! Thou art the ruins of the noblest man That ever lived in the tide of times. Woe to the hand that shed this costly blood!"

Blank Verse: Poetry written in iambic pentameter but unrhymed. Works by Shakespeare and Milton are epitomes of blank verse. Milton's *Paradise Lost* states, "Illumine, what is low raise and support, That to the heighth of this great argument I may assert Eternal Providence And justify the ways of God to men."

Caesura: A pause, usually signaled by punctuation, in a line of poetry. The earliest usage occurs in *Beowulf*, the first English epic dating from the Anglo-Saxon era. "To err is human, // to forgive, divine." (Pope).

Conceit: A whimsical or fancifully ingenious idea or an elaborate, startling, extravagant, or strained metaphor, usually in verse. John Donne's metaphysical poetry contains many clever conceits. For instance, Donne's "The Flea" (1633) compares a flea bite to the act of love; and in "A Valediction: Forbidding Mourning" (1633) separated lovers are likened to the legs of a compass, the leg drawing the circle eventually returning home to "the fixed foot."

Connotation: The ripple effect surrounding the implications and associations of a given word, distinct from the denotative, or literal meaning. For example, "Good night, sweet prince, and flights of angels sing thee to thy rest," refers to a burial.

Consonance: The repetition of similar consonant sounds, most often used in poetry. "Sally sat sifting seashells by the seashore" is a familiar example.

Couplet: Two rhyming lines of poetry. Shakespeare's sonnets end in heroic couplets written in iambic pentameter. Pope is also a master of the couplet. His *Rape of the Lock* is written entirely in heroic couplets.

Denotation: What a word literally means, as opposed to its connotative meaning. For example, *rose* means a flower of a certain species; however, it is often used connotatively to suggest beauty or even a beautiful woman.

Diction: The right word in the right spot for the right purpose. The hallmark of a great writer is precise, unusual, and memorable diction.

Epiphany: The moment when the proverbial light bulb goes off in one's head and comprehension sets in.

Exposition: Fill-in or background information about characters meant to clarify and add to the narrative; the initial plot element which precedes the buildup of conflict.

Figurative Language: Not meant in a literal sense but to be interpreted through symbolism. Figurative language is made up of such literary devices as hyperbole, metonymy, synecdoche, and oxymoron. A synecdoche is a figure of speech in which the word for part of something is used to mean the whole; for example, "sail" for "boat," or vice versa.

Free Verse: Poetry that does not have any predictable meter or patterning. Margaret Atwood, E. E. Cummings, and Ted Hughes write in this form.

Hyperbole: Exaggeration for a specific effect. For example, "I'm so hungry that I could eat a million of these."

Iambic Pentameter: The two elements in a set five-foot line of poetry. An iamb is two syllables, unaccented and accented, per foot or measure. Pentameter means five feet of these iambs per line or ten syllables.

Inversion: Typical English word order is reversed for a specific purpose. Bacon and Milton use inversion successfully. Emily Dickinson was fond of arranging words outside of their familiar order. For example in "Chartless" she writes "Yet know I how the heather looks" and "Yet certain am I of the spot." Instead of saying "Yet I know" and "Yet I am certain," she reverses the usual order and shifts the emphasis to the more important words.

Irony: An unexpected disparity between what is written or stated and what is really meant or implied by the author. Verbal, situational, and dramatic are the three literary ironies. Verbal irony is when an author says one thing but means something else. Dramatic irony is when an audience perceives something that a character in the literature does not know. Irony of situation is a discrepancy between the expected result and actual results. Shakespeare's plays contain numerous and highly effective use of irony. O.Henry's short stories have ironic endings.

Kenning: Another way to describe a person, place, or thing so as to avoid prosaic repetition. The earliest examples can be found in Anglo-Saxon literature such as *Beowulf* and "The Seafarer." Instead of writing "King Hrothgar," the anonymous monk wrote "great Ring-Giver," or "Father of his people." A lake becomes the swans' way, and the ocean or sea becomes the great whale's way. In ancient Greek literature, this device was called an "epithet."

Metaphysical Poetry: Verse characterization by ingenious wit, unparalleled imagery (often jarring), and clever conceits. The greatest metaphysical poet is John Donne. Henry Vaughn (and other 17th century British poets) contributed to this movement in *Words*, "I saw eternity the other night, like a great being of pure and endless light."

Metonymy: Use of an object or idea closely identified with another object or idea to represent the second. "Hit the books" means "go study." Washington, D.C. means the U.S. government and the White House means the U.S. President.

Motif: A key, oft-repeated phrase, name, or idea in a literary work. Dorset/Wessex in Hardy's novels and the moors and the harsh weather in the Bronte sisters' novels are effective use of motifs. Shakespeare's *Romeo and Juliet* represents the ill-fated young lovers' motif.

Onomatopoeia: Word used to evoke the sound in its meaning. The early Batman series used *pow, zap, whop, zonk* and *eek* in an onomatopoetic way.

Ottava rima: A specific eight-line stanza of poetry whose rhyme scheme is abababcc. Lord Byron's mock epic, *Don Juan*, is written in this poetic way.

Oxymoron: A contradictory form of speech, such as jumbo shrimp, unkindly kind, or singer John Mellencamp's "It hurts so good."

Paradox: Seemingly untrue statement, which when examined more closely proves to be true. John Donne's sonnet "Death Be Not Proud" postulates that death shall die and humans will triumph over death, at first thought not true, but ultimately explained and proven in this sonnet.

Parallelism: A type of close repetition of clauses or phrases that emphasize key topics or ideas in writing. The psalms in the King James Version of the *Bible* contain many examples.

Personification: Giving human characteristics to inanimate objects or concepts. Great writers, with few exceptions, are masters of this literary device.

Quatrain: A poetic stanza composed of four lines. A Shakespearean or Elizabethan sonnet is made up of three quatrains and ends with a heroic couplet.

Scansion: The two-part analysis of a poetic line. Count the number of syllables per line and determine where the accents fall. Divide the line into metric feet. Name the meter by the type and number of feet. Much is written about scanning poetry. Try not to inundate your students with this jargon; rather allow them to feel the power of the poets' words, ideas, and images instead.

Soliloquy: A highlighted speech, in drama, usually delivered by a major character expounding on the author's philosophy or expressing, at times, universal truths. This is done with the character alone on the stage.

Spenserian Stanza: Invented by Sir Edmund Spenser for *The Fairie Queene*, his epic poem honoring Queen Elizabeth I. Each stanza consists of nine lines, eight in iambic parameter. The ninth line, called an alexandrine, has two extra syllables or one additional foot.

Sprung Rhythm: Invented and used extensively by the poet Gerard Manley Hopkins. It consists of variable meter, which combines stressed and unstressed syllables fashioned by the author. See "Pied Beauty" or "God's Grandeur."

Stream of Consciousness: A style of writing that reflects the mental processes of the characters expressing, at times, jumbled memories, feelings, and dreams. Big time players in this type of expression are James Joyce, Virginia Woolf, and William Faulkner.

Terza Rima: A series of poetic stanzas utilizing the recurrent rhyme scheme of aba, bcb, cdc, ded, and so forth. The second-generation Romantic poets—Keats, Byron, Shelley, and, to a lesser degree, Yeats—used this Italian verse form, especially in their odes. Dante used this stanza in *The Divine Comedy*.

Tone: The discernible attitude inherent in an author's work regarding the subject, readership, or characters. Swift's or Pope's tone is satirical. Boswell's tone toward Johnson is admiring.

Wit: Writing of genius, keenness, and sagacity expressed through clever use of language. Alexander Pope and the Augustans wrote about and were themselves said to possess wit.

The more basic terms and devices, such as alliteration, allusion, analogy, aside, assonance, atmosphere, climax, consonance, denouement, elegy, foil, foreshadowing, metaphor, simile, setting, symbol, and theme are defined and exemplified in the English 5-9 Study Guide.

2. In analyzing non-literary written pieces, some of the same skills apply. For example, it's important to know what the point of the piece is. What did the writer intend to achieve? Consider the following:

"Consider the Alternatives: Alternative Fueled Vehicles and Alternative Vehicle Fuels

Driving a car fueled by something other than gasoline or diesel fuel is no longer the stuff of science fiction. In addition to conventional gasoline and diesel fuel, reformulated — cleaner — gasoline and alternative fuels now are sold in many parts of the country. Alternative fuels such as methanol, ethanol, compressed natural gas, liquefied petroleum gas, and electricity produce fewer tail pipe pollutants than conventional gasoline and diesel fuel. Using them could improve air quality.

Congress passed the Energy Policy Act in 1992 to promote the use of alternative fuels. For example, the law requires owners of fleet vehicles to purchase a certain number of alternative fueled vehicles. Congress also directed the Federal Trade Commission (FTC), the nation's consumer protection agency, to issue labeling requirements for alternative fuels and alternative fueled vehicles.

The Alternative Fuels and Vehicles (AFV) Rule and the Fuel Rating Rule require fuel dispensers and alternative fueled vehicles to be labeled with information to help consumers make knowledgeable decisions when it comes to filling up or buying a vehicle. The AFV Rule applies to new and used alternative fueled vehicles that are sold to consumers or leased to them for at least 120 days."

(http://www.ftc.gov/bcp/conline/pubs/autos/fuelffc.htm)

Structure: The first step in analyzing the structure of a piece of writing is to determine what the *point* is and where the writer has chosen to put it—at the beginning, some place in the middle, or at the end. In this case, the point of the paragraph is in the first sentence. The remainder provides supporting information. It tells of changes and innovations in what fuel is available now. It cites the Energy Policy Act of 1992 that is partly responsible for the increased availability of other fuels, and it lists some specifics about the Act that account for the changes that have taken place. Another way to look at the structure is in terms of whether the reasoning is inductive—moving from specific to general, or deductive—moving from general to specific. The reasoning in this paragraph is deductive. It starts with the generalization that cars fueled by something other than gasoline is a reality. Then it moves to specifics to make the point.

Content: Another important feature to analyze is the purpose of the paragraph. Is it persuasive—is the writer trying to persuade readers to switch fuels? Is it descriptive—does it try to appeal to the reader's senses—feel, touch, smell, hear, see? Is it narrative—does it tell a story? Or is it expository—does it merely give information that the reader might want, need, or be interested in? This is an expository paragraph. The purpose is to inform the reader about the use of alternative fuels. This writer doesn't concern himself with whether or not readers act on what he is writing or whether he stirs them emotionally. He simply wants to convey information. Another aspect to consider is whether or not there is bias. In order to make that judgment, we need to consider who the author is. In this case, we don't know the name of the writer, but we do know that the government is publishing it, so we can ask ourselves whether or not there is evidence of bias. Since the writing is expository, not persuasive, we might conclude that there is no bias. However, we should also consider whether this writer might have a reason to be biased, and we could conclude that the government might, in fact, have a possible ulterior motive in encouraging citizens to save on gasoline. Even so, there is no evidence in the writing, itself, to suggest that, so we must conclude that there is no bias here.

Skill 3.3   Identify the characteristics of emergent literacy.

The typical variation in literacy backgrounds that children bring to reading can make teaching more difficult. Often a teacher has to choose between focusing on the learning needs of a few students at the expense of the group or focusing on the group at the risk of leaving some students behind academically. This situation is particularly critical for children with gaps in their literacy knowledge who may be at risk in subsequent grades for becoming "diverse learners."

Areas of Emerging Evidence

• **Experiences with print (through reading and writing) help preschool children develop an understanding of the conventions, purpose, and functions of print.** Children learn about print from a variety of sources and in the process come to realize that print carries the story. They also learn how text is structured visually (i.e., text begins at the top of the page, moves from left to right, and carries over to the next page when it is turned). While knowledge about the conventions of print enables children to understand the physical structure of language, the conceptual knowledge that printed words convey a message also helps children bridge the gap between oral and written language.

A. **Phonological awareness and letter recognition contribute to initial reading acquisition by helping children develop efficient word recognition strategies (e.g., detecting pronunciations and storing associations in memory.)** Phonological awareness and knowledge of print-speech relations play an important role in facilitating reading acquisition. Therefore, phonological awareness instruction should be an integral component of early reading programs. Within the emergent literacy research, viewpoints diverged on whether acquisition of phonological awareness and letter recognition are preconditions of literacy acquisition or whether they develop interdependently with literacy activities such as story reading and writing.

• **Storybook reading affects children's knowledge about, strategies for, and attitudes towards reading.** Of all the strategies intended to promote growth in literacy acquisition, none is as commonly practiced, nor as strongly supported across the emergent literacy literature as storybook reading. Children in different social and cultural groups have differing degrees of access to storybook reading. For example, it is not unusual for a teacher to have students who have experienced thousands of hours of story reading time, along with other students who have had little or no such exposure.

Design Principles in Emergent Literacy

• **Conspicuous Strategies.** As an instructional priority, conspicuous strategies are a sequence of teaching events and teacher actions used to help students learn new literacy information and relate it to their existing knowledge. Conspicuous strategies can be incorporated in beginning reading instruction to ensure that all learners have basic literacy concepts. For example, during storybook reading teachers can show students how to recognize the fronts and backs of books, locate titles, or look at pictures and predict the story, rather than assume children will learn this through incidental exposure. Similarly, teachers can teach students a strategy for holding a pencil appropriately or checking the form of their letters against an alphabet sheet on their desks or the classroom wall.

- **Mediated Scaffolding.** Mediated scaffolding can be accomplished in a number of ways to meet the needs of students with diverse literacy experiences. To link oral and written language, for example, teachers may use texts that simulate speech by incorporating oral language patterns or children's writing. Or teachers can use daily storybook reading to discuss book-handling skills and directionality-concepts that are particularly important for children who are unfamiliar with printed texts. Teachers can also use repeated readings to give students multiple exposures to unfamiliar words or extended opportunities to look at books with predictable patterns, as well as provide support by modeling the behaviors associated with reading. Teachers can act as *scaffolds* during these storybook reading activities by adjusting their demands (e.g., asking increasingly complex questions or encouraging children to take on portions of the reading) or by reading more complex text as students gain knowledge of beginning literacy components.

- **Strategic Integration.** Many children with diverse literacy experiences have difficulty making connections between old and new information. Strategic integration can be applied to help link old and new learning. For example, in the classroom, strategic integration can be accomplished by providing access to literacy materials in classroom writing centers and libraries. Students should also have opportunities to integrate and extend their literacy knowledge by reading aloud, listening to other students read aloud, and listening to tape recordings and videotapes in reading corners.

Primed Background Knowledge. All children bring some level of background background knowledge (e.g., how to hold a book, awareness of directionality of print) to beginning reading. Teachers can utilize children's background knowledge to help children link their personal literacy experiences to beginning reading instruction, while also closing the gap between students with rich and students with impoverished literacy experiences. Activities that draw upon background knowledge include incorporating oral language activities (which discriminate between printed letters and words) into daily read-alouds, as well as frequent opportunities to retell stories, look at books with predictable patterns, write messages with invented spellings, and respond to literature through drawing.

Emergent literacy research examines early literacy knowledge and the contexts and conditions that foster that knowledge. Despite differing viewpoints on the relation between emerging literacy skills and reading acquisition, strong support was found in the literature for the important contribution that early childhood exposure to oral and written language makes to the facility with which children learn to read.

Other References

Ehri, L. C., & Sweet, J. (1991). Fingerpoint-reading of memorized text: What enables beginners to process the print? *Reading Research Quarterly*, 26(4), 442-462.

Hiebert, E. H., & Papierz, J. M. (1990). The emergent literacy construct and kindergarten and readiness books of basal reading series. *Early Childhood Research Quarterly*, 5(3), 317-334.

Morrow, L. M. (1990). Preparing the classroom environment to promote literacy during play. *Early Childhood Research Quarterly*, 5, 537-554.

Morrow, L. M., O'Connor, E. M., & Smith, J. K. (1990). Effects of a story reading program on the literacy development of at-risk kindergarten children. *Journal of Reading Behavior*, 22(3), 255-275.

Roberts, B. (1992). The evolution of the young child's concept of word as a unit of spoken and written language. *Reading Research Quarterly*, 27(2), 125-138.

Stahl, S. A., & Miller, P. D. (1989). Whole language and language experience approaches for beginning reading: A quantitative research synthesis. *Review of Educational Research*, 59(1), 87-116.

van Kleeck, A. (1990). Emergent literacy: Learning about print before learning to read. *Topics in Language Disorders*, 10(2), 25-45.

Skill 3.4   Identify methods for determining students' reading ability.

Skills to Evaluate:

- Ability to use syntactic cues when encountering an unknown word. A good reader will expect the word to fit the syntax he/she is familiar with. A poor reader may substitute a word that does not fit the syntax, and will not correct him/herself.
- Ability to use semantic cues to determine the meaning of an unknown word. A good reader will consider the meanings of all the known words in the sentence. A poor reader may read one word at a time with no regard for the other words.
- Ability to use schematic cues to connect words read with prior knowledge. A good reader will incorporate what he/she knows with what the text says or implies. A poor reader may think only of the word he/she is reading without associating it with prior knowledge.

- Ability to use phonics cues to improve ease and efficiency in reading. A good reader will apply letter and sound associations almost subconsciously. A poor reader may have one of two kinds of problems: he/she may have underdeveloped phonics/skills, and use only an initial clue without analyzing vowel patterns before quickly guessing the word. Or he/she may use phonics skills in isolation, becoming so absorbed in the word "noises" that he/she ignores or forgets the message of the text.
- Ability to process information from text. A student should be able to get information from the text as well as store, retrieve, and integrate it for later use.
- Ability to use interpretive thinking to make logical predictions and inferences.
- Ability to use critical thinking to make decisions and insights about the text.
- Ability to use appreciative thinking to respond to the text, whether emotionally, mentally, ideologically, etc.

Methods of Evaluation:

- Assess students at the beginning of each year to determine grouping for instruction.
- Judge whether a student recognizes when a word does not make sense.
- Monitor whether the student corrects him/herself—if he/she knows when to ignore and read on or when to reread a sentence.
- Look for skills such as recognizing cause and effect, finding main ideas, and using comparison and contrast techniques.
- Use oral reading to assess reading skills. Pay attention to word recognition skills rather than the reader's ability to communicate the author's message. Strong oral reading sounds like natural speech, utilizes phrasing and pace that match the meaning of the text, and uses pitch and tone to interpret the text.
- Keep dated records to follow individual progress. Focus on a few students each day. Grade them on a scale of 1-5 according to how well they perform certain reading abilities (e.g. logically predict coming events). Also include informal observations, such as "Ed was able to determine the meaning of the word 'immigrant' by examining the other words in the sentence."
- Remember that evaluation is important, but enjoyment of reading is the most important thing to emphasize. Keep reading a pressure-free, fun activity so students do not become intimidated by reading. Even if students are not meeting excellence standards, if they continue wanting to read each day, that is a success!

Skill 3.5   Identify strategies for using students' first language in their development of literacy in English as a second language.

Students who are raised in homes where English is not the first language and/or where standard English is not spoken may have difficulty with hearing the difference between similar sounding words like "send" and "sent." Any student who is not in a home environment where English phonology operates may have difficulty perceiving and demonstrating the differences between English language phonemes. If students cannot hear the difference between words that sound the same like "grow" and "glow," they will be confused when these words appear in a print context. This confusion will, of course, impact their comprehension.

Considerations for teaching English Language Learners include recognition by the teacher that what works for the English-language-speaking student from an English-language-speaking family does not necessarily work in other languages.

ELL students should learn to read initially in their first languages. It has been found that a priority for ELL should be learning to speak English before being taught to read English because oral language development lays the foundation for phonological awareness.

Skill 3.6   Identify strategies for using students' prior knowledge, experiences, and culture for literacy development.

Reading emphasis in middle school

Reading for comprehension of factual material—content textbooks, reference books, and newspapers—is closely related to study strategies in middle/junior high. Organized study models, such as the SQ3R method, a technique that makes it possible and feasible to learn the content of even large amounts of text (Survey, Question, Read, Recite, and Review Studying), teach students to locate main ideas and supporting details, to recognize sequential order, to distinguish fact from opinion, and to determine cause/effect relationships.

Strategies

1. Teacher-guided activities that require students to organize and to summarize information based on the author's explicit intent are pertinent strategies in middle grades. Evaluation techniques include oral and written responses to standardized or teacher-made worksheets.

2. Reading of fiction introduces and reinforces skills in inferring meaning from narration and description. Teaching-guided activities in the process of reading for meaning should be followed by cooperative planning of the skills to be studied and of the selection of reading resources. Many printed reading-for-comprehension instruments as well as individualized computer software programs are available to facilitate the monitoring of the progress in acquisition of comprehension skills.

3. Older middle-school students should be given opportunities for more student centered activities—individual and collaborative selection of reading choices based on student interest, small-group discussions of selected works and greater written expression. Evaluation techniques include teacher monitoring and observation of discussions and written work samples.

4. Certain students may begin some fundamental critical interpretation—recognizing fallacious reasoning in news media, examining the accuracy of news reports and advertising, or explaining their reasons for preferring one author's writing over another's. Development of these skills may require a more learning-centered approach in which the teacher identifies a number of objectives and suggested resources from which the student may choose his course of study. Self-evaluation through a reading diary should be stressed. Teacher and peer evaluation of creative projects resulting from such study is encouraged.

5. Reading aloud before the entire class as a formal means of teacher evaluation should be phased out in favor of one-to-one tutoring or peer-assisted reading. Occasional sharing of favored selections by both teacher and willing students is a good oral-interpretation basic.

COMPETENCY 4.0 KNOWLEDGE OF CONTENT AND STRATEGIES FOR TEACHING INTEGRATED LANGUAGE ARTS

Skill 4.1   Identify variations in language across contexts and cultures.

The content in material to be presented orally plays a big role in how it is organized and delivered. For example, a literary analysis or a book report will be organized inductively, laying out the details and then presenting a conclusion, which will usually be what the author's purpose, message, and intent are. If the analysis is focusing on multiple layers in a story, that will probably follow the preliminary conclusion. On the other hand, keeping in mind that the speaker will want to keep the audience's attention, if the content has to do with difficult-to-follow facts and statistics, slides (or PowerPoint) may be used as a guide to the presentation, and the speaker will intersperse interesting anecdotes, jokes, or humor from time to time so the listeners don't fall asleep.

It's also important to take the consistency of the audience into account when organizing a presentation. If the audience can be counted on to have a high level of interest in what is being presented, little would need to be done in the way of organizing and presenting to hold interest. On the other hand, if many of those in the audience are there because they have to be, or if the level of interest can be counted on not to be very high, something like a PowerPoint presentation can be very helpful. Also the lead-in and introduction need to be structured not only to be entertaining and interest-grabbing, it should create an interest in the topic. If the audience members are senior citizens, it's important to keep the presentation lively and to be careful not to "speak down" to them. Carefully written introductions aimed specifically at this audience will go a long way to attract their interest in the topic.

No speaker should stand up to make a presentation if the purpose has not been carefully determined ahead of time. If the speaker is not focused on the purpose, the audience will quickly lose interest. As to organizing for a particular purpose, some of the decisions to be made are where it will occur in the presentation—beginning, middle, or end—and whether displaying the purpose on a chart, PowerPoint, or banner will enhance the presentation. The purpose might be the lead-in for a presentation if it can be counted on to grab the interest of the listeners, in which case, the organization will be deductive. If it seems better to save the purpose until the end, the organization, of course, will be inductive.

The occasion, of course, plays an important role in the development and delivery of a presentation. A celebration speech when the company has achieved an important accomplishment will be organized around congratulating those who were most responsible for the accomplishment and giving some details about how it was achieved and probably something about the competition for the achievement. The presentation will be upbeat and not too long.

On the other hand, if bad news is being presented, it will probably be the CEO who is making the presentation and the bad-news announcement will come first followed with details about the news itself and how it came about, and probably end with a pep talk and encouragement to do better the next time.

"Political correctness" is a new concept tossed around frequently in the 21st century. It has always existed, of course. The successful speaker of the 19th century understood and was sensitive to audiences. However, that person was typically a man, of course, and the only audience that was important was a male audience, and more often than not, the only important audience was a white one.

Many things have changed in discourse since the 19th century just as the society the speaker lives in and addresses has changed, and the speaker who disregards the existing conventions for "political correctness" usually finds himself/herself in trouble. Rap music makes a point of ignoring those conventions, particularly with regard to gender, and is often the target of very hostile attacks. On the other hand, rap performers often intend to be revolutionary and have developed their own audiences and have become outrageously wealthy by exploiting those newly-developed audiences based primarily on thumbing their noses at establishment conventions.

Even so, the successful speaker must understand and be sensitive to what is current in "political correctness." The "n word" is a case in point. There was a time when that term was thrown about at will by politicians and other public speakers, but no more. Nothing could spell the end of a politician's career more certainly than using that term in his campaign or public addresses.

These terms are called "pejorative"—A word or phrase that expresses contempt or disapproval. Such terms as *redneck*, *queer*, or *cripple* may only be considered pejorative if used by a non-member of the group they apply to. For example, the "n word," which became very inflammatory in the 1960s, is now being used sometimes by African-American artists to refer to themselves, especially in their music, with the intention of underscoring their protest of the establishment.

References to gender have became particularly sensitive in the 20th century as a result of the women's rights movement, and the speaker who disregards these sensitivities does so at his/her peril. The generic "he" is no longer acceptable, and this requires a strategy to deal with pronominal references without repetitive he/she, his/her, etc. Several ways to approach this: switch to a passive construction that does not require a subject; switch back and forth, using the male pronoun in one reference and the female pronoun in another one, being sure to sprinkle them reasonably evenly; or switch to the plural. The last alternative is the one most often chosen. This requires some care, and the speaker should spend time developing these skills before stepping in front of an audience.

Dialect differences are basically in pronunciation. Bostoners say "pahty" for "party" and Southerners blend words like "you all" into "y'all." Besides the dialect differences already mentioned, the biggest geographical factors in American English stem from minor word choice variances. Depending on the region where you live, when you order a carbonated, syrupy beverage most generically called a soft drink, you might ask for a "soda" in the South, or a "pop" in the Midwest. If you order a soda in New York, then you will get a scoop of ice cream in your soft drink, while in other areas you would have to ask for a "float."

Skill 4.2   Identify individual and peer activities that support the reading and writing processes.

Viewing writing as a process allows teachers and students to see the writing classroom as a cooperative workshop where students and teachers encourage and support each other in each writing endeavor. Listed below are some techniques that help teachers to facilitate and create a supportive classroom environment.

1. Create peer response/support groups that are working on similar writing assignments. The members help each other in all stages of the writing process-from prewriting, writing, revising, editing, and publishing.

2. Provide several prompts to give students the freedom to write on a topic of their own. Writing should be generated out of personal experience and students should be introduced to in-class journals. One effective way to get into writing is to let them write often and freely about their own lives, without having to worry about grades or evaluation.

3. Respond in the form of a question whenever possible. Teacher/facilitator should respond noncritically and use positive, supportive language.

4. Respond to formal writing acknowledging the student's strengths and focusing on the composition skills demonstrated by the writing. A response should encourage the student by offering praise for what the student has done well. Give the student a focus for revision and demonstrate that the process of revision has applications in many other writing situations.

5. Provide students with readers' checklists so they can write observational critiques of others' drafts, and then they can revise their own papers at home using the checklists as a guide.

6. Pair students so that they can give and receive responses. Pairing students keeps them aware of the role of an audience in the composing process and in evaluating stylistic effects.

7. Focus critical comments on aspects of the writing that can be observed in the writing. Comments like "I noticed you use the word 'is' frequently" will be more helpful than "Your introduction is dull" and will not demoralize the writer.

8. Provide the group with a series of questions to guide them through the group writing sessions.

Skill 4.3 **Identify appropriate selections from the genres of literature, including adolescent literature.**

The major literary genres include those listed below:

Allegory: A story in verse or prose with characters representing virtues and vices. Allegories may be read on either of two levels, the literal and the symbol. John Bunyan's The Pilgrim's Progress is the most renowned of this genre.

Autobiography: A form of the biography written by the subject himself or herself. Autobiographies can range from very formal works, to intimate journals and diaries in the course of a life, without a conscious eye toward publication.

Ballad: An *in medias res* story told or sung, usually in verse and accompanied by music. Literary devices found in ballads include the refrain, or repeated section, and incremental repetition, or anaphora, for effect. Earliest forms were anonymous folk ballads.

Biography: A portrait of the life of an individual other than oneself. Biographical prose is a subcategory of nonfiction. The earliest biographical writings were probably funeral speeches and inscriptions, usually praising the life and example of the deceased. Early biographies evolved from this and were almost invariably uncritical, even distorted, and always laudatory.

Drama: Plays- comedy, modern, or tragedy - typically in five acts. Traditionalists and neoclassicists adhere to Aristotle's unities of time, place, and action. Modern playwrights have taken the form and broken it up as they please. Plot development is advanced via dialogue. Common dramatic devices include asides, soliloquies, and a chorus representing public opinion. Greatest of all dramatists/playwrights is William Shakespeare. Other greats include Ibsen, Williams, Miller, Shaw, Stoppard, Racine, Moliére, Sophocles, Aeschylus, Euripides, and Aristophanes.

Epic: A long poem usually of book length reflecting values inherent in the generative culture. Devices include the invocation of a Muse for inspiration; prologue expounding in a purpose in writing; universal setting; protagonist and antagonist who possess supernatural strength and acumen, and interventions of a God or the gods. Understandably, there are very few epics: Homer's Iliad and Odyssey, Virgil's Aeneid, Milton's Paradise Lost, Spenser's The Fairie Queene, Barrett Browning's Aurora Leigh, and Pope's mock-epic, The Rape of the Lock are some examples.

Epistle: A letter that is not always originally intended for public distribution; yet, owing to the fame of its sender or recipient, it becomes public domain. Paul wrote epistles that were later placed in the Bible.

Essay: Typically a limited length prose work focusing on a topic and propounding a definite point of view and authoritative tone. Great essayists include Carlyle, Lamb, DeQuincy, Emerson, and Montaigne, who is credited with defining this genre.

Fable: Terse tale offering up a moral or exemplum. Chaucer's "The Nun's Priest's Tale" is a fine example of a bete fabliau, or beast fable, in which animals speak and act characteristically human, illustrating human foibles.

Informational books and articles: Make up much of the reading of modern Americans. Magazines began to be popular in the 19th century in this country, and while many of the contributors to those publications intended to influence the political/social/religious convictions of their readers, many also simply intended to pass on information. A book or article whose purpose is simply to be informative, that is, not to persuade, is called exposition. An example of an expository book is the MLA Style Manual. The writers do not intend to persuade their readers to use the recommended stylistic features in their writing; they are simply making them available in case a reader needs such a guide.

Legend: A traditional narrative or collection of related narratives, popularly regarded as historically factual but actually a mixture of fact and fiction.

Myth: Stories that are more or less universally shared within a culture to explain its history and traditions.

Newspaper accounts of events: Expository in nature, of course, a reporting of a happening. That happening might be a school board meeting, an automobile accident that sent several people to a hospital and accounted for the death of a passenger, or the election of the mayor. Although presented with in the mannerisms of the objective viewpoint, they invariably contain the biases of the reporter, and the periodical or newspaper in which they appear. Even news stories headline some facts and omit others, and by so doing they slant their stories to emphasize certain aspects of the truth over others. Today, with digital photography and computer generated graphics, the story in the pictorial layout also influences the audience, and is the choice of the paper's editorial board. Reporters are expected to be unbiased in their coverage, and most of them will defend their disinterest fiercely, but what a writer sees in an event is inevitably shaped to some extent by the writer's beliefs and experiences.

Novel: The longest form of fictional prose containing a variety of characterizations, settings, local color, and regionalism. Most have complex plots, expanded description, and attention to detail. Some of the great novelists include Austin, Twain, Tolstoy, Hugo, Hardy, Dickens, Hawthorne, Forster, and Flaubert.

Poem: The only requirement is rhythm. Poetry evolved from oral literature and folk tale as a written form with set patterns, and in English Literature, which in English literature include the sonnet, elegy, ode, pastoral, and villanelle. Unfixed variations on traditional forms have trickled through blank verse and the dramatic monologue. From Modernism to the modern day they have transverse experiments with typography—Imagisme—and Self-revelatory themes—Confessional poetry.

Romance: A highly imaginative tale set in a fantastical realm dealing with the conflicts between heroes, villains, and/or monsters. "The Knight's Tale" from Chaucer's Canterbury Tales and Keats' "The Eve of St. Agnes" are prime representatives.

Short Story: Typically a terse narrative with less developmental background about characters. Short stories may include description, author's point of view, and tone. Poe emphasized that a successful short story should create one focused impact. Considered to be great short story writers are Hemingway, Faulkner, Twain, Joyce, Shirley Jackson, Flannery O'Connor, de Maupasssant, Saki, Edgar Allen Poe, and Pushkin.

Dramatic Texts

Comedy: The comedic form of dramatic literature is meant to amuse and often ends happily. It uses techniques such as satire or parody and can take many forms, from farce to burlesque.

Tragedy: Tragedy is comedy's other half. It is defined as a work of drama written in either prose or poetry, telling the story of a brave, noble hero who, because of some tragic character flaw, brings ruin upon himself. It is characterized by serious, poetic language that evokes pity and fear. In modern times, dramatists have tried to update its image by drawing its main characters from the middle class and showing their nobility through their nature instead of their standing.

Drama: In its most general sense, a drama is any work that is designed to be performed by actors onstage. It can also refer to the broad literary genre that includes comedy and tragedy. Contemporary usage, however, denotes drama as a work that treats serious subjects and themes but does not aim for the same grandeur as tragedy. Drama usually deals with characters of a less stately nature than tragedy.

Dramatic Monologue: A dramatic monologue is a speech given by an actor, usually intended for themselves, but with the intended audience in mind. It reveals key aspects of the character's psyche and sheds insight on the situation at hand. The audience takes the part of the silent listener, passing judgment and giving sympathy at the same time. This form was invented and used predominantly by Victorian poet Robert Browning.

Recognize a wide range of literature and other texts appropriate for students

Adolescent literature, because of the age range of readers, is extremely diverse. Fiction for the middle group, usually ages ten/eleven to fourteen/fifteen, deals with issues of coping with internal and external changes in their lives. Because children's writers in the twentieth century have produced increasingly realistic fiction, adolescents can now find problems dealt with honestly in novels.

Teachers of middle/junior high school students see the greatest change in interests and reading abilities. Fifth and sixth graders, included in elementary grades in many schools, are viewed as older children while seventh and eighth graders are preadolescent. Ninth graders, included sometimes as top dogs in junior high school and sometimes as underlings in high school, definitely view themselves as teenagers. Their literature choices will often be governed more by interest than by ability; thus, the wealth of high-interest, low readability books that have flooded the market in recent years. Tenth through twelfth graders will still select high-interest books for pleasure reading but are also easily encouraged to stretch their literature muscles by reading more classics.

Because of the rapid social changes, topics that once did not interest young people until they reached their teens - suicide, gangs, homosexuality - are now subjects of books for even younger readers. The plethora of high-interest books reveals how desperately schools have failed to produce on-level readers and how the market has adapted to that need. However, these high-interest books are now readable for younger children whose reading levels are at or above normal. No matter how tastefully written, some contents are inappropriate for younger readers.

The problem becomes not so much steering students toward books that they have the reading ability to handle, but encouraging them toward books whose content is appropriate to their levels of cognitive and social development. A fifth-grader may be able to read V.C. Andrews book Flowers in the Attic but not possess the social/moral development to handle the deviant behavior of the characters. At the same time, because of the complex changes affecting adolescents, the teacher must be well versed in learning theory and child development as well as competent to teach the subject matter of language and literature.

For sixth graders

Barrett, William. Lilies of the Field
Cormier, Robert. Other Bells for Us to Ring
Dahl, Roald. Danny, Champion of the World; Charlie and the Chocolate Factory
Lindgren, Astrid. Pippi Longstocking
Lindbergh, Anne. Three Lives to Live
Lowry, Lois. Rabble Starkey
Naylor, Phyllis. The Year of the Gopher, Reluctantly Alice
Peck, Robert Newton. Arly
Speare, Elizabeth. The Witch of Blackbird Pond
Sleator, William. The Boy Who Reversed Himself

For seventh and eighth grades

Most seventh and eight grade students, according to learning theory, are still functioning cognitively, psychologically, and morally as sixth graders. As these are not inflexible standards, there are some twelve and thirteen year olds who are much more mature socially, intellectually, and physically than the younger children who share the same school. They are becoming concerned with establishing individual and peer group identities that presents conflicts with breaking from authority and the rigidity of rules. Some at this age are still tied firmly to the family and its expectations, while others identify more with those their own age or older.

Enrichment reading for this group must help them cope with life's rapid changes or provide escape and thus must be either realistic or fantastic depending on the child's needs. Adventures and mysteries (the Hardy Boys and Nancy Drew series) are still popular today. These preteens also become more interested in biographies of contemporary figures rather than legendary figures of the past.

Reading level 7.0 to 7.9

Armstrong, William. Sounder
Bagnold, Enid. National Velvet
Barrie, James. Peter Pan
London, Jack. White Fang, Call of the Wild
Lowry, Lois. Taking Care of Terrific
McCaffrey, Anne. The Dragonsinger series
Montgomery, L. M. Anne of Green Gables and sequels
Steinbeck, John. The Pearl
Tolkien, J. R. R. The Hobbit
Zindel, Paul. The Pigman

Reading level 8.0 to 8.9

Cormier, Robert. I Am the Cheese
McCullers, Carson. The Member of the Wedding
North, Sterling. Rascal
Twain, Mark. The Adventures of Tom Sawyer

For ninth grade

Depending upon the school system, a ninth grader may be top-dog in a junior high school or underdog in a high school. Much of his social development and thus his reading interests become motivated by his peer associations. He is technically an adolescent operating at the early stages of formal operations in cognitive development. His perception of his own identity is becoming well-defined and he is fully aware of the ethics required by society. He is more receptive to the challenges of classic literature but still enjoys popular teen novels.

Reading level 9.0 to 9.9

> Brown, Dee. *Bury My Heart at Wounded Knee*
> Defoe, Daniel. *Robinson Crusoe*
> Dickens, Charles. *David Copperfield*
> Greenberg, Joanne. *I Never Promised You a Rose Garden*
> Kipling, Rudyard. *Captains Courageous*
> Mathabane, Mark. *Kaffir Boy*
> Nordhoff, Charles. *Mutiny on the Bounty*
> Shelley, Mary. *Frankenstein*
> Washington, Booker T. *Up From Slavery*

For tenth - twelfth grades

All high school sophomores, juniors, and seniors can handle most other literature except for a few of the very most difficult titles like *Moby Dick* or *Vanity Fair*. However, since many high school students do not progress to the eleventh- or twelfth-grade reading level, they will still have their favorites among authors whose writings they can understand. Many will struggle with assigned novels but still read high-interest books for pleasure. A few high-interest titles are listed below without reading level designations, though most are 6.0 to 7.9.

> Bauer, Joan. *Squashed*
> Borland, Hal. *When the Legends Die*
> Danzinger, Paula. *Remember Me to Herald Square*
> Duncan, Lois. *Stranger with my Face*
> Hamilton, Virginia. *The Planet of Junior Brown*
> Hinton, S. E. *The Outsiders*
> Paterson, Katherine. *The Great Gilly Hopkins*

Teachers of students at all levels must be familiar with the materials offered by the libraries in their own schools. Only then can they guide their students into appropriate selections for their social age and reading-level development.

Skill 4.4 **Determine effective strategies for teaching students reading, speaking, listening, and viewing for various purposes.**

Preparing to speak on a topic should be seen as a process that has stages: **Discovery**, **Organization**, and **Editing**.

Discovery: There are many possible sources for the information that will be used to create an oral presentation. The first step in the discovery process is to settle on a topic or subject. Answer the question, what is the speech going to be about? For example, the topic or subject could be immigration. In the discovery stage, one's own knowledge, experience, and beliefs should be the first source, and notes should be taken as the speaker probes this source. The second source can very well be interviews with friends and possibly experts. The third source will be research: what has been written or said publicly on this topic. This stage can get out of hand very quickly, so a plan for the collecting of source information should be well-organized with time limits set for each part.

Organization: At this point, several decisions need to be made. The first is what the *purpose* of the speech is. Does the speaker want to persuade the audience to believe something or to act on something, or does the speaker simply want to present information that the audience might not have? Once that decision is made, a thesis should be developed. What point does the speaker want to make? And what are the points that will support that point? And in what order will those points be arranged? Introductions and conclusions should be written last. The purpose of the introduction is to draw the audience into the topic. The purpose of the conclusion is to polish off the speech, making sure the thesis is clear, reinforcing the thesis, or summarizing the points that have been made.

Editing: This is the most important stage in preparing a speech. Once decisions have been made in the discovery and organization stages, it's good to allow time to let the speech rest for awhile and to go back to it with "fresh eyes." Objectivity is extremely important, and the speaker should be willing to make drastic changes if they are needed. It's difficult to turn loose of one's own composition, but good speech-makers are able to do that. On the other hand, this can also get out of hand, and it should be limited. The speaker must recognize that at some point, the decisions must be made, the die must be cast, commitment to the speech as it stands must be made if the speaker is to deliver the message with conviction.

The concept of recursiveness is very useful to one who writes speeches. That is, everything must be written at the outset with full knowledge that it can be changed, and the willingness to go backward, even to the discovery stage, is what makes a good speech-writer.

The more information a speaker has about an audience, the more likely he/she is to communicate effectively with them. Several factors figure into the speaker/audience equation: age, ethnic background, educational level, knowledge of the subject, and interest in the subject.

Speaking about computers to senior citizens who have, at best, rudimentary knowledge about the way computers work must take that into account. Perhaps handing out a glossary would be useful for this audience. Speaking to first-graders about computers presents its own challenges. On the other hand, the average high-school student has more experience with computers than most adults and that should be taken into account. Speaking to a room full of computer systems engineers requires a rather thorough understanding of the jargon related to the field.

In considering the age of the audience, it's best not to make assumptions. The gathering of senior citizens might include retired systems engineers or people who have made their livings using computers, so research about the audience is important. It might not be wise to assume that high-school students have a certain level of understanding, either.

With an audience that is primarily Hispanic with varying levels of competence in English, the speaker is obligated to adjust the presentation to fit that audience.

The same would be true when the audience is composed of people who may have been in the country for a long time but whose families speak their first language at home. Black English presents its own peculiarities, and if the audience is composed primarily of African-Americans whose contacts in the larger community are not great, some efforts need to be made to acquaint oneself with the specific peculiarities of the community those listeners come from.

It's unwise to "speak down" to an audience; they will almost certainly be insulted. On the other hand, speaking to an audience of college graduates will require different skills than speaking to an audience of people who have never attended college.

Finally, has the audience come because of an interest in the topic or because they have been influenced or forced to come to the presentation? If the audience comes with an interest in the subject already, efforts to motivate or draw them into the discussion might not be needed. On the other hand, if the speaker knows the audience does not have a high level of interest in the topic, it would be wise to use devices to draw them into it, to motivate them to listen.

Slang comes about for many reasons: Amelioration is an important one that results often in euphemisms. Examples are "passed away" for dying; "senior citizens" for old people. Some usages have become so embedded in the language that their sources are long-forgotten. For example, "fame" originally meant rumor. Some words that were originally intended as euphemisms such as "mentally retarded" and "moron" to avoid using "idiot" have themselves become pejorative.

Slang is lower in prestige than Standard English; tends to first appear in the language of groups with low status; is often taboo and unlikely to be used by people of high status; and tends to displace conventional terms, either as a shorthand or as a defense against perceptions associated with the conventional term.

Informal and formal language is a distinction made on the basis of the occasion as well as the audience. At a "formal" occasion, for example, a meeting of executives or of government officials, even conversational exchanges are likely to be more formal. A cocktail party or a golf game are examples where the language is likely to be informal. Formal language uses fewer or no contractions, less slang, longer sentences, and more organization in longer segments.

Speeches delivered to executives, college professors, government officials, etc., is likely to be formal. Speeches made to fellow employees are likely to be informal. Sermons tend to be formal; Bible lessons will tend to be informal.

Jargon is a specialized vocabulary. It may be the vocabulary peculiar to a particular industry such as computers or of a field such as religion. It may also be the vocabulary of a social group. Black English is a good example. A Hardee's ad has two young men on the streets of Philadelphia discussing the merits of one of their sandwiches, and bylines are required so others may understand what they're saying. A whole vocabulary that has even developed its own dictionaries is the jargon of bloggers. The speaker must be knowledgeable about and sensitive to the jargon peculiar to the particular audience. That may require some research and some vocabulary development on the speaker's part.

Technical language is a form of jargon. It is usually specific to an industry, profession, or field of study. Sensitivity to the language familiar to the particular audience is important.

Regionalisms are those usages that are peculiar to a particular part of the country. A good example is the second person plural pronoun: you. Because the plural form is identical to that of the singular, various parts of the country have developed their own solutions to be sure that they are understood when they are speaking to more than one "you." In the South, "you-all" or "y'all" is common. In the Northeast, one often hears "youse." In some areas of the Middlewest, "you'ns" can be heard.

Vocabulary also varies from region to region. A small stream is a "creek" in some regions but "crick" in some. In Boston, soft drinks are generically called "tonic," but it becomes "soda" in other parts of the northeast. It is "liqueur" in Canada, and "pop" when you get very far west of New York.

Oral use of communication forms

Different from the basic writing forms of discourse is the art of debating, discussion, and conversation. The ability to use language and logic to convince the audience to accept your reasoning and to side with you is an art. This form of writing/speaking is extremely confined/structured, logically sequenced, with supporting reasons and evidence. At its best, it is the highest form of propaganda. A position statement, evidence, reason, evaluation, and refutation are integral parts of this writing schema.

Interviewing provides opportunities for students to apply expository and informative communication. It teaches them how to structure questions to evoke fact-filled responses. Compiling the information from an interview into a biographical essay or speech helps students to list, sort, and arrange details in an orderly fashion.

Speeches that encourage them to describe persons, places, or events in their own lives or oral interpretations of literature help them sense the creativity and effort used by professional writers.

Communication skills are crucial in a collaborative society. In particular, a person cannot be a successful communicator without being an active listener. Focus on what others say, rather than planning on what to say next. By listening to everything another person is saying, you may pick up on natural cues that lead to the next conversation move without so much added effort.

Facilitating
It is quite acceptable to use standard opening lines to facilitate a conversation. Don't agonize over trying to come up with witty "one-liners," as the main obstacle in initiating conversation is just getting the first statement over with. After that, the real substance begins. A useful technique may be to make a comment or ask a question about a shared situation. This may be anything from the weather, to the food you are eating, to a new policy at work. Use an opener you are comfortable with, because most likely, your partner in conversation will be comfortable with it as well.

Stimulating Higher Level Critical Thinking Through Inquiry
Many people rely on questions to communicate with others. However, most fall back on simple clarifying questions rather than open-ended inquiries. Try to ask open-ended, deeper-level questions, since those tend to have the greatest reward and lead to a greater understanding. In answering those questions, more complex connections are made and more significant realizations are achieved.

Voice: Many people fall into one of two traps when speaking: using a monotone, or talking too fast. These are both caused by anxiety. A monotone restricts your natural inflection but can be remedied by releasing tension in upper and lower body muscles. Subtle movement will keep you loose and natural. Talking too fast, on the other hand, is not necessarily a bad thing if the speaker is exceptionally articulate. If not, though, or if the speaker is talking about very technical things, it becomes far too easy for the audience to become lost. When you talk too fast and begin tripping over your words, consciously pause after every sentence you say. Don't be afraid of brief silences. The audience needs time to absorb what you are saying.

The successful conversationalist is a person who keeps up with what's going on in the world both far and near and ponders the meanings of events and developments. That person also usually reads about the topics that are of the most interest to him, both in printed materials and online. In addition, the effective conversationalist has certain areas that are of particular interest that have been probed in some depth. An interest in human behavior is usually one of this person's most particular interests. Why do people behave as they do? Why do some succeed and some fail? This person will also be interested in and concerned about social issues, particularly in the immediate community but also on a wider scale and will have ideas for solving some of those problems.

With all of this, the most important thing a good conversationalist can do is to *listen*, not just wait until the other person quits speaking so he or she can take the floor again but actually listen to learn what the other person has to say and also to learn more about that other person. Following a gathering, the best thing a person can think about another is that he or she was interested enough to listen to the other's ideas and opinions, and that is the person who will be remembered the longest and with the most regard.

It's acceptable to be passionate about one's convictions in polite conversation; it is not acceptable to be overbearing or unwilling to hear and consider another's point of view. It's important to keep one's emotions under control in these circumstances even if the other person does not.

Debates and panel discussions fall under the umbrella of formal speaking, and the rules for formal speaking should apply here although lapsing into conversational language is acceptable. Swear words should be avoided in these situations.

A debate presents two sides of a debatable thesis—pro and con. Each side will posit a hypothesis, prove it, and defend it. A formal debate is a sort of formal dance with each side following a strictly defined format. However, within those guidelines, debaters are free to develop their arguments and rebuttals as they choose. The successful debater prepares by developing very thoroughly both sides of the thesis: "Mexico's border with the United States must be closed" and "Mexico's border with the United States must remain open." Debaters must be thoroughly prepared to argue their own side, but they must also have a strategy for rebutting the opposing side's arguments. All aspects of critical thinking and logical argument are employed, and the successful debaters will use ethical appeal (their own credibility) and emotional appeal to persuade the judges who will determine who wins—that is, the side that best establishes its thesis, proves it logically, but also *persuades* the audience to come over to its position.

A panel is typically composed of *experts* who explain and defend a particular topic. Often, panels will include representatives from more than one field of study and more than one position on the topic.
Typically, each will have a limited amount of time to make an opening statement either presenting explanatory material or arguing a point of view. Then the meeting will be opened up to the audience for questions. A moderator will keep order and will control the time limits on the opening statements and responses and will sometimes intervene and ask a panel member that was not the target of a particular question from the audience to elaborate or rebut the answer of the panel member who was questioned. Panels are usually limited to four or five people although in special cases, they may be much larger.

Volume: Problems with volume, whether too soft or too loud, can usually be combated with practice. If you tend to speak too softly, have someone stand in the back of the room and give you a signal when your volume is strong enough. If possible, have someone in the front of the room as well to make sure you're not overcompensating with excessive volume. Conversely, if you have a problem with speaking too loudly, have the person in the front of the room signal you when your voice is soft enough and check with the person in the back to make sure it is still loud enough to be heard. In both cases, note your volume level for future reference. Don't be shy about asking your audience, "Can you hear me in the back?" Suitable volume is beneficial for both you and the audience.

Pitch: Pitch refers to the length, tension, and thickness of a person's vocal bands. As your voice gets higher, the pitch gets higher. In oral performance, pitch reflects upon the emotional arousal level. More variation in pitch typically corresponds to more emotional arousal but can also be used to convey sarcasm or highlight specific words.

Posture: Maintain a straight, but not stiff posture. Instead of shifting weight from hip to hip, point your feet directly at the audience and distribute your weight evenly. Keep shoulders orientated towards the audience. If you have to turn your body to use a visual aid, turn 45 degrees and continue speaking toward the audience.

Movement: Instead of staying glued to one spot or pacing back and forth, stay within four to eight feet of the front row of your audience, and take maybe a step or half-step to the side every once in a while. If you are using a lectern, feel free to move to the front or side of it to engage your audience more. Avoid distancing yourself from the audience; you want them to feel involved and connected.

Gestures: Gestures are a great way to maintain a natural atmosphere when speaking publicly. Use them just as you would when speaking to a friend. They shouldn't be exaggerated, but they should be utilized for added emphasis. Avoid keeping your hands in your pockets or locked behind your back, wringing your hands and fidgeting nervously, or keeping your arms crossed.

Eye Contact: Many people are intimidated by using eye contact when speaking to large groups. Interestingly, eye contact usually *helps* the speaker overcome speech anxiety by connecting with an attentive audience and easing feelings of isolation. Instead of looking at a spot on the back wall or at your notes, scan the room and make eye contact for one to three seconds per person.

Multimedia refers to a technology for presenting material in both visual and verbal forms. This format is especially conducive to the classroom, since it reaches both visual and auditory learners.

Knowing how to select effective teaching software is the first step in efficient multi-media education. First, decide what you need the software for (creating spreadsheets, making diagrams, creating slideshows, etc.) Consult magazines such as *Popular Computing, PC World, MacWorld,* and *Multimedia World* to learn about the newest programs available. Go to a local computer store and ask a customer service representative to help you find the exact equipment you need. If possible, test the programs you are interested in. Check reviews in magazines such as *Consumer Reports, PCWorld, Electronic Learning* or *MultiMedia Schools* to ensure the software's quality.

Software programs useful for producing teaching material
- Adobe
- Aldus Freehand
- CorelDRAW!
- DrawPerfect
- Claris Works
- PC Paintbrush
- Harvard Graphics

- Visio
- Microsoft Word
- Microsoft Power Point

Tips for using print media and visual aids
- Use pictures over words whenever possible.
- Present one key point per visual.
- Use no more than 3-4 colors per visual to avoid clutter and confusion.
- Use contrasting colors such as dark blue and bright yellow.
- Use a maximum of 25-35 numbers per visual aid.
- Use bullets instead of paragraphs when possible.
- Make sure it is student-centered, not media-centered. Delivery is just as important as the media chosen.

Tips for using film and television
- Study programs in advance.
- Obtain supplementary materials such as printed transcripts of the narrative or study guides.
- Provide your students with background information, explain unfamiliar concepts, and anticipate outcomes.
- Assign outside readings based on their viewing.
- Ask cuing questions.
- Watch along with students.
- Observe students' reactions.
- Follow up viewing with discussions and related activities.

Tips for creating visual media
- Limit your graph to just one idea or concept
- Keep the content simple and concise (avoid too many lines, words, or pictures)
- Balance substance and visual appeal
- Make sure the text is large enough for the class to read
- Match the information to the format that will fit it best

Skill 4.5   **Identify appropriate methods and materials for meeting the learning needs of diverse students.**

Research is beginning to document the ways in which minority parents interact with their children that support learning yet differ from more mainstream or middle-class approaches. One recent study explored the non-traditional ways Hispanic parents tend to be involved in their children's education, which are not necessarily recognized by educators as parent involvement. Further research is needed to delve deeply into the connections that diverse families create that traditional indicators do not recognize and to consider the reasons why some diverse families might not be involved in the more traditional ways. Building a body of knowledge about the specific practices of various cultural groups can support the validation of those practices by school personnel and may support the sharing of effective practices across cultural groups.

Interactive homework assignments: The development of interactive homework assignments (homework that requires parent-child interaction as part of the activity) has shown promise as a way of supporting parent involvement and student achievement. Homework activities that are explicitly designed to encourage interaction between parents and children have shown positive results for increasing achievement in several subject areas, including science and language arts.

Well-designed interactive assignments can have a number of positive outcomes: they can help students practice study skills, prepare for class, participate in learning activities, and develop personal responsibility for homework as well as promote parent-child relations, develop parent-teacher communication, and fulfill policy directives from administrators.

School support of parental homework help: Although parents express positive feelings about homework, they have concerns about homework, their personal limitations in subject-matter knowledge, and effective helping strategies. More research is needed on how school personnel can effectively support parental homework help.

Skill 4.6   **Identify effective strategies for analyzing and evaluating print and non-print messages for meaning, method, and intent.**

More money is spent each year on advertising toward children than educating them. Thus, the media's strategies are considerably well-thought-out and effective. They employ large, clear letters, bold colors, simple line drawings, and popular symbols to announce upcoming events, push ideas and advertise products. By using attractive photographs, brightly colored cartoon characters or instructive messages, they increase sales, win votes or stimulate learning. The graphics are designed to communicate messages clearly, precisely, and efficiently. Some even target subconscious yearnings for sex and status.

Because so much effort is being spent on influencing students through media tactics, just as much effort should be devoted to educating those students about media awareness. A teacher should explain that artists and the aspect they choose to portray, as well as the ways in which they portray them, reflect their attitude and understanding of those aspects. The artistic choices they make are not entirely based on creative license—they also reflect an imbedded meaning the artist wants to represent. Colors, shapes, and positions are meant to arouse basic instincts for food, sex, and status, and are often used to sell cars, clothing, or liquor.

To stimulate analysis of media strategies, ask students such questions as:

* Where/when do you think this picture was taken/film was shot/piece was written?
* Would you like to have lived at this time in history, or in this place?
* What objects are present?
* What do the people presented look like? Are they happy or sad?
* Who is being targeted?
* What can you learn from this piece of media?
* Is it telling you something is good or bad?
* What message is being broadcast?

Skill 4.7 Identify strategies for teaching students to write for a variety of purposes and audiences.

In the past teachers have assigned reports, paragraphs and essays that focused on the teacher as the audience with the purpose of explaining information. However, for students to be meaningfully engaged in their writing, they must write for a variety of reasons. Writing for different audiences and aims allows students to be more involved in their writing. If they write for the same audience and purpose, they will continue to see writing as just another assignment.

Listed below are suggestions that give students an opportunity to write in more creative and critical ways.

* Write letters to the editor, to a college, to a friend, or to another student that would be sent to the intended audience.
* Write stories that would be read aloud to a group (the class, another group of students, to a group of elementary school students) or published in a literary magazine or class anthology.
* Write plays that would be performed.
* Have students discuss the parallels between the different speech styles we use and writing styles for different readers or audiences.
* Allow students to write a particular piece for different audiences.
* Make sure students consider the following when analyzing the needs of their audience.

- ✓ Why is the audience reading my writing? Do they expect to be informed, amused, or persuaded?
- ✓ What does my audience already know about my topic?
- ✓ What does the audience want or need to know? What will interest them?
- ✓ What type of language suits my readers?
- As part of the prewriting, have students identify the audience.
- Expose students to writing that is on the same topic but with a different audience and have them identify the variations in sentence structure and style.

Remind your students that it is not necessary to identify all the specifics of the audience in the initial stage of the writing process but that at some point they must make some determinations about audience:

- **Values**—What is important to this group of people? What is their background and how will that affect their perception of your speech?
- **Needs**—Find out in advance what the audience's needs are. Why are they listening to you? Find a way to satisfy their needs.
- **Constraints**—What might hold the audience back from being fully engaged in what you are saying, or agreeing with your point of view, or processing what you are trying to say? These could be political reasons, which make them wary of your presentation's ideology from the start, or knowledge reasons, in which the audience lacks the appropriate background information to grasp your ideas. Avoid this last constraint by staying away from technical terminology, slang, or abbreviations that may be unclear to your audience.
- **Demographic Information**—Take the audience's size into account, as well as the location of the presentation.

Start where the listeners are, and then take them where you want to go!

Listening to students sitting on the steps that lead into the building that houses their classrooms, teachers will hear dialogue that may not even be understandable to them. The student who is writing to his peers will need to know and understand the peculiarities of that discourse in order to be very effective with them. This is a good example for students of what it means to tailor language for a particular audience and for a particular person.

This is a good time to teach the concept of jargon. Writing to be read by a lawyer is a different thing from writing to be read by a medical doctor. Writing to be read by parents is different from writing to be read by the administrator of the school. Not only are the vocabularies different, but the formality/informality of the discourse will need to be adjusted.

The things to be aware of in determining what the language should be for a particular audience, then, hinges on two things: vocabulary and formality/informality. The most formal language does not use contractions or slang. The most informal language will certainly use contractions and the slang that is appropriate for the particular audience. Formal language will use longer sentences and will not sound like a conversation. The most informal language will use shorter sentences—not necessarily simple sentences—but shorter constructions and will sound like a conversation.

Novels use formal language only when it is in the mouth of a character who would speak that way, such as a lawyer or a school superintendent. It's jarring to read a novel that has a construction worker using formal language. Using examples of various characters and their dialogues from fiction is useful in helping students understand this crucial aspect of writing.

Journalistic Writing

News reporters generally become excellent writers because they get a lot of practice, which is a principle most writing teachers try to employ with their students. Also, news writing is instructive in skills for writing clearly and coherently.

Reporters generally write in one of two modes: straight reporting and feature writing. In both modes, the writer must be concerned with accuracy and objectivity. The reporter does not write his opinions. He/she does not write persuasive discourse. The topic is typically assigned although some experienced reporters have the opportunity to seek out and develop their own stories.

Investigative reporting is sometimes seen as a distinct class although, technically, all reporters are "investigative." That is, they research the background of the story they're reporting, using as many means as are available. For example, the wife of a conservative, model minister murders him premeditatively and in cold blood. The reporter reports the murder and the arrest of the wife, but the story is far from complete until some questions are answered, the most obvious one being "why?" The reporter is obligated to try to answer that question and to do so will interview as many people as will talk to him about the lives of both minister and wife, their parents, members of the church, their neighbors, etc. The reporter will also look at newspaper archives in the town where the murder took place as well as in newspapers in any town the husband and/or wife has lived in previously. High-school yearbooks are a source that are often explored in these cases.

When Bob Woodward and Carl Bernstein, reporters for *The Washington Post,* began to break the Watergate story in 1972 and 1973, they set new standards for investigative reporting and had a strong influence on journalistic writing. Most reporters wanted to be Woodward and Bernstein and became more aggressive than reporters had been in the past. Even so, the basic techniques and principles still apply. The reporting of these two talented journalists demonstrated that while newspapers keep communities aware of what's going on, they also have the power to influence it.

A good news story is written as an "inverted pyramid." That is, the reasoning is deductive. The "thesis" or point is stated first and is supported with details. It reasons from general (the broad top of the inverted triangle) to specific. The lead sentence might be, "The body of John Smith was found in the street in front of his home with a bullet wound through his skull." The headline will be a trimmed-down version of that sentence and shaped to grab attention. It might read: "Murdered man found on Spruce Street." The news article might fill several columns, the first details having to do with the finding of the body, the next the role of the police; the third will spread out and include details about the victim's life, then the scope will broaden to details about his family, friends, neighbors, etc. If he held a position of prominence in the community, those details will broaden further and include information about his relationships to fellow-workers and his day-to-day contacts in the community. The successful reporter's skills include the ability to do thorough research, to maintain an objective stance (not to become involved personally in the story), and to write an effective "inverted pyramid."

Feature writing is more like an informative essay although it may also follow the inverted pyramid model. This form of reporting focuses on a topic designed to be interesting to at least one segment of the readership—possible sports enthusiasts, travelers, vacationers, families, women, food lovers, etc. The article will focus on one aspect of the area of interest such as a particular experience for the vacationing family. The first sentence might read something like this: "Lake Lure offers a close-to-home relaxing weekend getaway for families in East Tennessee." The development can be an ever-widening pyramid of details focused particularly on what the family can experience at Lake Lure but also directions for how to get there.

While the headline is intended to contain in capsule form the point that an article makes, it is rarely written by the reporter. This can sometimes result in a disconnection between headline and article. Well-written headlines will provide a guide for the reader as to what is in the article; they will also be attention-grabbers. This requires a special kind of writing, quite different from the inverted pyramid that distinguishes these writers from the investigative or feature reporter.

Other Forms of Expository Writing

It may seem sometimes that the **business letter** is a thing of the past. Although much business-letter writing has been relegated to email communications, letters are still a potentially valuable form of communication. A carefully-written letter can be powerful. It can alienate, convince, persuade, entice, motivate, and/or create good-will.

As with any other communication, it's worthwhile to learn as much as possible about the receiver. This may be complicated if there will be more than one receiver of the message; in these cases, it's best to aim for the lowest common denominator if that can be achieved without "writing down" to any of those who will read and be affected or influenced by the letter. It may be better to send more than one form of the letter to the various receivers in some cases.

Purpose is the most powerful factor in writing a business letter. What is the letter expected to accomplish? Is it intended to get the receiver to act or to act in a specific manner? Are you hoping to see some action take place as the result of the letter? If so, you should clearly define for yourself what the purpose is before you craft the letter, and it's good to include a time deadline for the response.

Reasons for choosing the letter as the channel of communication include the following:

1. It's easy to keep a record of the transaction.
2. The message can be edited and perfected before it is transmitted.
3. It facilitates the handling of details.
4. It's ideal for communicating complex information.
5. It's a good way to disseminate mass messages at a relatively low cost.

The parts of a business letter are as follow: date line, inside address, salutation, subject line*, body, complimentary close, company name*, signature block, reference initials*, enclosure notation*, copy notation*, and postscript*.
*not required but sometimes useful.

Business letters typically use formal language. They should be straightforward and courteous. The writing should be concise, and special care should be taken to leave no important information out. Clarity is very important; otherwise, it may take more than one exchange of letters or phone calls to get the message across.

A complaint is a different kind of business letter. It can come under the classification of a "bad news" business letter, and there are some guidelines that are helpful when writing this kind of letter. A positive writing style can overcome much of the inherent negativity of a letter of complaint. No matter how much in the right you may be, maintaining self-control and courtesy and avoiding demeaning or blaming language is more likely to be effective. Abruptness, condescension, or harshness of tone will not help achieve your purpose, particularly if you are requesting a positive response such as reimbursement for a bad product or some help in righting a wrong that may have been done to you. It's important to remember that you want to solve the specific problem and to retain the good will of the receiver if possible.

Induction is better than deduction for this type of communication. Beginning with the details and building to the statement of the problem generally has the effect of softening the bad news. It's also useful to begin with an opening that will serve as a buffer. The same is true for the closing. It's good to leave the reader with a favorable impression by writing a closing paragraph that will generate good will rather than bad.

A formal essay, on the other hand, may be persuasive, informative, descriptive, or narrative in nature. The purpose should be clearly defined, and development must be coherent and easy to follow.

Email has revolutionized business communications. It has most of the advantages of business letters and the added ones of immediacy, lower costs, and convenience. Even very long reports can be attached to an email. On the other hand, a two-line message can be sent and a response received immediately bringing together the features of a postal system and the telephone. Instant messaging goes even one step further. It can do all of the above—send messages, attach reports, etc.—and still have many of the advantages of a telephone conversation.

Email has an unwritten code of behavior that includes restrictions on how informal the writing can be. The level of accepted business conversation is usually also acceptable in emails. Capital letters and bolding are considered shouting and are usually frowned on.

Skill 4.8 **Identify strategies for teaching usage, mechanics, spelling, and vocabulary in the writing process.**

Identification of common morphemes, prefixes, and suffixes

This aspect of vocabulary development is to help students look for structural elements within words which they can use independently to help them determine meaning.

The terms listed below are generally recognized as the key structural analysis components.

Root words: A root word is a word from which another word is developed. The second word can be said to have its "root" in the first. This structural component nicely lends itself to a tree with roots illustration which can concretize the meaning for students. Students may also want to literally construct root words using cardboard trees and/or actual roots from plants to create word family models. This is a lovely way to help students own their root words.

Base words: A stand-alone linguistic unit which cannot be deconstructed or broken down into smaller words. For example, in the word "re-tell," the base word is "tell."

Contractions: These are shortened forms of two words in which a letter or letters have been deleted and replaced by an apostrophe.

Prefixes: These are beginning units of meaning the can be added (the vocabulary word for this type of structural adding is "affixed") to a base word or root word. They can not stand alone. They are also sometimes known as "bound morphemes," meaning that they cannot stand alone as a base word.

Suffixes: These are ending units of meaning which can be "affixed" or added on to the *ends* of root or base words. Suffixes transform the original meanings of base and root words. Like prefixes, they are also known as "bound morphemes," because they can not stand alone as words.

Compound words: These occur when two or more base words are connected to form a new word. The meaning of the new word is in some way connected with that of the base word.

Inflectional endings: Are suffixes that impart a new meaning to the base or root word. These endings in particular change the gender, number, tense, or form of the base or root words.

Sentence completeness

A sentence is a structure that has a subject and a predicate. If it has a subject and a predicate but also has an element that makes it dependent on another sentence, it is said to be a clause. Some examples:
because he ate it all has a subject and a predicate but is an adverb clause signaled by the introductory "because." It could function as an adverb clause in the following sentence: The freezer contains no ice cream *because he ate it all.*
for whom the bell tolls has a subject and predicate but is a noun clause because of the introductory "for whom." It could function as a noun in the following sentence: I know *for whom the bell tolls.*

It's vital to teach students the structure of the English sentence if they are to recognize such things as fragments (a clause acting as a sentence) or run-on sentences (independent sentences jammed up against one another without proper coordination or punctuation).

Sentence structure

A simple sentence has one subject and one predicate. A compound sentence is two sentences (either simple, compound, or complex) joined by a conjunction (and, or, for, yet, but, so). The appropriate punctuation for a compound sentence is as follows: If the two simple sentences are short, no punctuation is required; however, if the sentences are longer, a comma may be used for clarification.

Example: *The children were playing, and their mothers were watching them.*

A complex sentence is a simple sentence with one or more modifying clauses such as an adverb clause, an adjective clause, or a noun clause.

Examples:
A. Complex sentence with an adverb clause:
   The freezer has no ice cream because he ate all of it. One way to identify an adverb clause is by whether it can be moved from the back to the front of the sentence without changing meaning: *Because he ate all of it, the freezer has no ice cream.*
   Proper punctuation for this construction: If the clause appears at the end of the main sentence, no punctuation is required; if it appears at the beginning of the sentence, before the main sentence, it must be set off with a comma.
B. Complex sentence with an adjective clause:
   The man who came to dinner stayed all night. "who came to dinner" modifies *man* and is, therefore an adjective clause.
   Punctuation: If the adjective clause is restrictive, it requires no punctuation; if it is nonrestrictive, it must be set off with commas to denote its nonrestrictive nature.
C. Complex sentence with a noun clause:
   I know for whom the bell tolls. "for whom the bell tolls" is functioning as the object of the verb "know" in this sentence; therefore, it is a noun clause.
   Punctuation: noun clauses require no punctuation.

Parallelism

Recognize parallel structures using phrases (prepositional, gerund, participial, and infinitive) and omissions from sentences that create the lack of parallelism.

Prepositional phrase/single modifier

Incorrect: Coleen ate the ice cream with enthusiasm and hurriedly.
Correct: Coleen ate the ice cream with enthusiasm and in a hurry.
Correct: Coleen ate the ice cream enthusiastically and hurriedly.

Participial phrase/infinitive phrase

Incorrect: After hiking for hours and to sweat profusely, Joe sat down to rest and drinking water.
Correct: After hiking for hours and sweating profusely, Joe sat down to rest and drink water.

Recognition of dangling modifiers

Dangling phrases are attached to sentence parts in such a way they create ambiguity and incorrectness of meaning.

Participial phrase

Incorrect: Hanging from her skirt, Dot tugged at a loose thread.
Correct: Dot tugged at a loose thread hanging from her skirt.

Incorrect: Relaxing in the bathtub, the telephone rang.
Correct: While I was relaxing in the bathtub, the telephone rang.

Infinitive phrase

Incorrect: To improve his behavior, the dean warned Fred.
Correct: The dean warned Fred to improve his behavior.

Prepositional phrase

Incorrect: On the floor, Father saw the dog eating table scraps.
Correct: Father saw the dog eating table scraps on the floor.

Recognition of syntactical redundancy or omission

These errors occur when superfluous words have been added to a sentence or key words have been omitted from a sentence.

Redundancy

Incorrect: Joyce made sure that when her plane arrived that she retrieved all of her luggage.
Correct: Joyce made sure that when her plane arrived she retrieved all of her luggage.

Incorrect: He was a mere skeleton of his former self.
Correct: He was a skeleton of his former self.

Omission

Incorrect: Dot opened her book, recited her textbook, and answered the teacher's subsequent question.
Correct: Dot opened her book, recited from the textbook, and answered the teacher's subsequent question.

Avoidance of double negatives

This error occurs from positioning two negatives that, in fact, cancel each other in meaning.

Incorrect: Harold couldn't care less whether he passes this class.
Correct: Harold could care less whether he passes this class.

Incorrect: Dot didn't have no double negatives in her paper.
Correct: Dot didn't have any double negatives in her paper.

Types of Clauses

Clauses are connected word groups that are composed of *at least* one subject and one verb. (A subject is the doer of an action or the element that is being joined. A verb conveys either the action or the link.)

Students are waiting for the start of the assembly.
Subject   Verb

At the end of the play, students wait for the curtain to come down.
                    Subject   Verb

Clauses can be independent or dependent.

Independent clauses can stand alone or can be joined to other clauses.

Independent clause   for
                                and
                                nor

Independent clause,	but or yet so	Independent clause
Independent clause	;	Independent clause
Dependent clause	,	Independent clause
Independent clause		Dependent clause

Dependent clauses, by definition, contain at least one subject and one verb. However, they cannot stand alone as a complete sentence. They are structurally dependent on the main clause.

There are two types of dependent clauses: (1) those with a subordinating conjunction, and (2) those with a relative pronoun

Sample subordinating conjunctions:
Although
When
If
Unless
Because

Unless a cure is discovered, many more people will die of the disease.
     Dependent clause   +   Independent clause

Sample relative pronouns:
Who
Whom
Which
That

The White House has an official website, which contains press releases, news updates, and biographies of the President and Vice-President.
(Independent clause + relative pronoun + relative dependent clause)

Misplaced and Dangling Modifiers

Particular phrases that are not placed near the one word they modify often result in misplaced modifiers. Particular phrases that do not relate to the subject being modified result in dangling modifiers.

Error: Weighing the options carefully, a decision was made regarding the punishment of the convicted murderer.

Problem: Who is weighing the options? No one capable of weighing is named in the sentence; thus, the participle phrase weighing the options carefully dangles. This problem can be corrected by adding a subject of the sentence capable of doing the action.

Correction: Weighing the options carefully, the judge made a decision regarding the punishment of the convicted murderer.

Error: Returning to my favorite watering hole, brought back many fond memories.

Problem: The person who returned is never indicated, and the participle phrase dangles. This problem can be corrected by creating a dependent clause from the modifying phrase.

Correction: When I returned to my favorite watering hole, many fond memories came back to me.

Error: One damaged house stood only to remind townspeople of the hurricane.

Problem: The placement of the misplaced modifier only suggests that the sole reason the house remained was to serve as a reminder. The faulty modifier creates ambiguity.

Correction: Only one damaged house stood, reminding townspeople of the hurricane.

Spelling

Concentration in this section will be on spelling plurals and possessives. The multiplicity and complexity of spelling rules based on phonics, letter doubling, and exceptions to rules - not mastered by adulthood - should be replaced by a good dictionary. As spelling mastery is also difficult for adolescents, our recommendation is the same. Learning the use of a dictionary and thesaurus will be a more rewarding use of time.

Most plurals of nouns that end in hard consonants or hard consonant sounds followed by a silent e are made by adding s. Some words ending in vowels only add s.

fingers, numerals, banks, bugs, riots, homes, gates, radios, bananas

Nouns that end in soft consonant sounds s, j, x, z, ch, and sh, add es. Some nouns ending in o add es.

dresses, waxes, churches, brushes, tomatoes, potatoes

Nouns ending in *y* preceded by a vowel just add *s*.

> boys, alleys

Nouns ending in *y* preceded by a consonant change the *y* to *i* and add *es*.

> babies, corollaries, frugalities, poppies

Some nouns plurals are formed irregularly or remain the same.

> sheep, deer, children, leaves, oxen

Some nouns derived from foreign words, especially Latin, may make their plurals in two different ways - one of them Anglicized. Sometimes, the meanings are the same; other times, the two plurals are used in slightly different contexts. It is always wise to consult the dictionary.

> appendices, appendixes   criterion, criteria
> indexes, indices   crisis, crises

Make the plurals of closed (solid) compound words in the usual way except for words ending in *ful* which make their plurals on the root word.

> timelines, hairpins, cupsful

Make the plurals of open or hyphenated compounds by adding the change in inflection to the word that changes in number.

> fathers-in-law, courts-martial, masters of art, doctors of medicine

Make the plurals of letters, numbers, and abbreviations by adding *s*.

fives and tens, IBMs, 1990s, *p*s and *q*s (Note that letters are italicized.)

Capitalization

Capitalize all proper names of persons (including specific organizations or agencies of government); places (countries, states, cities, parks, and specific geographical areas); and things (political parties, structures, historical and cultural terms, and calendar and time designations); and religious terms (any deity, revered person or group, sacred writings).

> Percy Bysshe Shelley, Argentina, Mount Rainier National Park,
> Grand Canyon, League of Nations, the Sears Tower, Birmingham,
> Lyric Theater, Americans, Midwesterners, Democrats, Renaissance,
> Boy Scouts of America, Easter, God, Bible, Dead Sea Scrolls, Koran

Capitalize proper adjectives and titles used with proper names.

California gold rush, President John Adams, French fries, Homeric epic, Romanesque architecture, Senator John Glenn

Note: Some words that represent titles and offices are not capitalized unless used with a proper name.

Capitalized	Not Capitalized
Congressman McKay	the congressman from Florida
Commander Alger	commander of the Pacific Fleet
Queen Elizabeth	the queen of England

Capitalize all main words in titles of works of literature, art, and music. (See "Using Italics" in the Punctuation section.)

The candidate should be cognizant of proper rules and conventions of punctuation, capitalization, and spelling. Competency exams will generally test the ability to apply the more advanced skills; thus, a limited number of more frustrating rules is presented here. Rules should be applied according to the American style of English, i.e. spelling *theater* instead of *theatre* and placing terminal marks of punctuation almost exclusively within other marks of punctuation.

Punctuation

Using terminal punctuation in relation to quotation marks

In a quoted statement that is either declarative or imperative, place the period inside the closing quotation marks.

> "The airplane crashed on the runway during takeoff."

If the quotation is followed by other words in the sentence, place a comma inside the closing quotations marks and a period at the end of the sentence.

> "The airplane crashed on the runway during takeoff," said the announcer.

In most instances in which a quoted title or expression occurs at the end of a sentence, the period is placed before either the single or double quotation marks.

> "The middle school readers were unprepared to understand Bryant's poem 'Thanatopsis.'"

> Early book-length adventure stories like *Don Quixote* and *The Three Musketeers* were known as "picaresque novels."

There is an instance in which the final quotation mark would precede the period - if the content of the sentence were about a speech or quote so that the understanding of the meaning would be confused by the placement of the period.

> The first thing out of his mouth was "Hi, I'm home."
> *but*
> The first line of his speech began "I arrived home to an empty house".

In sentences that are interrogatory or exclamatory, the question mark or exclamation point should be positioned outside the closing quotation marks if the quote itself is a statement or command or cited title.

> Who decided to lead us in the recitation of the "Pledge of Allegiance"?
>
> Why was Tillie shaking as she began her recitation, "Once upon a midnight dreary..."?
>
> I was embarrassed when Mrs. White said, "Your slip is showing"!

In sentences that are declarative but the quotation is a question or an exclamation, place the question mark or exclamation point inside the quotation marks.

> The hall monitor yelled, "Fire! Fire!"
>
> "Fire! Fire!" yelled the hall monitor.
>
> Cory shrieked, "Is there a mouse in the room?" (In this instance, the question supersedes the exclamation.)

Using periods with parentheses or brackets

Place the period inside the parentheses or brackets if they enclose a complete sentence, independent of the other sentences around it.

> Stephen Crane was a confirmed alcohol and drug addict. (He admitted as much to other journalists in Cuba.)

If the parenthetical expression is a statement inserted within another statement, the period in the enclosure is omitted.

> Mark Twain used the character Indian Joe (He also appeared in *The Adventures of Tom Sawyer*) as a foil for Jim in *The Adventures of Huckleberry Finn*.

When enclosed matter comes at the end of a sentence requiring quotation marks, place the period outside the parentheses or brackets.

"The secretary of state consulted with the ambassador [Albright]."

Using commas

Separate two or more coordinate adjectives, modifying the same word and three or more nouns, phrases, or clauses in a list.

Maggie's hair was dull, dirty, and lice-ridden.

Dickens portrayed the Artful Dodger as skillful pickpocket, loyal follower of Fagin, and defendant of Oliver Twist.

Ellen daydreamed about getting out of the rain, taking a shower, and eating a hot dinner.

In Elizabethan England, Ben Johnson wrote comedy, Christopher Marlowe wrote tragedies, and William Shakespeare composed both.

Use commas to separate antithetical or complimentary expressions from the rest of the sentence.

The veterinarian, not his assistant, would perform the delicate surgery.

The more he knew about her, the less he wished he had known.

Randy hopes to, and probably will, get an appointment to the Naval Academy.

His thorough, though esoteric, scientific research could not easily be understood by high school students.

Using double quotation marks with other punctuation

Quotations - whether words, phrases, or clauses - should be punctuated according to the rules of the grammatical function they serve in the sentence.

The works of Shakespeare, "the bard of Avon," have been contested as originating with other authors.

"You'll get my money," the old man warned, "when 'Hell freezes over'."

Sheila cited the passage that began "Four score and seven years ago...." (Note the ellipsis followed by an enclosed period.)

"Old Ironsides" inspired the preservation of the U.S.S. Constitution.

Use quotation marks to enclose the titles of shorter works: songs, short poems, short stories, essays, and chapters of books. (See "Using Italics" for punctuating longer titles.)

"The Tell-Tale Heart"   "Casey at the Bat"   "America the Beautiful"

Using semicolons

Use semicolons to separate independent clauses when the second clause is introduced by a transitional adverb. (These clauses may also be written as separate sentences, preferably by placing the adverb within the second sentence.)

The Elizabethans modified the rhyme scheme of the sonnet; thus, it was called the English sonnet.
or
The Elizabethans modified the rhyme scheme of the sonnet. It thus was called the English sonnet.

Use semicolons to separate items in a series that are long and complex or have internal punctuation.

The Italian Renaissance produced masters in the fine arts: Dante Alighieri, author of the *Divine Comedy;* Leonardo da Vinci, painter of *The Last Supper;* and Donatello, sculptor of the *Quattro Coronati,* the four saints.

The leading scorers in the WNBA were Haizhaw Zheng, averaging 23.9 points per game; Lisa Leslie, 22; and Cynthia Cooper, 19.5.

Using colons

Place a colon at the beginning of a list of items. (Note its use in the sentence about Renaissance Italians in the paragraph above.)

The teacher directed us to compare Faulkner's three symbolic novels: *Absalom, Absalom; As I Lay Dying;* and *Light in August.*

Do **not** use a comma if the list is preceded by a verb.

Three of Faulkner's symbolic novels are *Absalom, Absalom; As I Lay Dying,* and *Light in August.*

Using dashes

Place dashes to denote sudden breaks in thought.

> Some periods in literature - the Romantic Age, for example -
> spanned different time periods in different countries.

Use dashes instead of commas if commas are already used elsewhere in the
sentence for amplification or explanation.

> The Fireside Poets included three Brahmans - James Russell
> Lowell, Henry David Wadsworth, Oliver Wendell Holmes -
> and John Greenleaf Whittier.

Use italics to punctuate the titles of long works of literature, names of periodical
publications, musical scores, works of art and motion picture television, and radio
programs. (When unable to write in italics, students should be instructed to
underline in their own writing where italics would be appropriate.)

> *The Idylls of the King*   *Hiawatha*   *The Sound and the Fury*
> *Mary Poppins*   *Newsweek*   *The Nutcracker Suite*

**Skill 4.9   Identify strategies for incorporating multicultural experiences
in reading and writing activities in the integrated language
arts.**

Teachers have a critical role to play in encouraging multicultural experiences.
They have an opportunity to incorporate activities that reflect our nation's
increasing diversity and allow students to share their similarities, develop a
positive cultural identity, and appreciate the unique contributions of all cultures.

The best way to incorporate multicultural literature, depicting African-American,
Asian, Arabic, Native American, and Hispanic heritage, is to integrate it into the
established reading program rather than as a separate or distinct area of study.

Reading Workshops

In reading workshops, students select from a variety of reading materials such as books, biographies, encyclopedias, and magazines. Students share their responses to the literature by writing or talking with teachers and classmates. It allows students to take ownership of their reading by choosing their own reading material. Teachers need to have a large supply of multicultural literature to choose from that is sensitive to and reflective of students' diverse cultural backgrounds. When reading these materials, students can learn that most people have similar emotions, needs and dreams. During reading workshops, students usually engage in reading, responding, sharing, and reading aloud.

Reading. Students usually need an hour when they can independently read books and other written materials that include diverse cultures. Classrooms should have a variety of instructional materials representing diverse cultures.

Responding. After students read a multicultural storybook, teachers should direct the students to reflect on the meaning of the story in their own lives. In this process, students interpret meanings and draw inferences based upon their own cultural perspectives and experiences. Students might keep journals in which they write their initial responses to the materials they are reading. They may also talk with the teacher about their books. Teachers should help students move beyond simply writing summaries and toward reflecting and making connections between literature and their own lives.

Sharing. Sharing differences of diverse families heightens a child's sensitivity to issues involving prejudice, racism, and intolerance toward students of different cultures. Exposing students to culturally diverse literature provides them with a means to become global citizens who can perform more effectively in a culturally diverse society.

Reading Aloud. Teachers read aloud when they wish to present literature that students might not be able to read themselves, such as classics that they feel every student should be exposed to. Students should participate in a class discussion about the book, share the reading experience, and respond to the story together as a community of learners, not as individuals.

Writing Workshops

It is important for teachers to encourage students to write stories depicting the lives of persons around the world as they imagine a setting and characters with foreign names. In a writing workshop, students can make a box containing cultural items of a country or several countries such as ornaments, clothing, pictures, or music tapes associated with the story line they create.

Another way of integrating multicultural activities in a writing workshop is to involve students in a pen-pal project. Students can compose group letters to partner classes in other nations about their school, their lives, or a favorite part of the books they have read about the partner's country. Copies of these books and thank-you notes from partner classes can be displayed in the school by posting them on bulletin boards. From this activity, students learn that there are interesting books to read from different countries and nice kids to share ideas with all around the world. As students engage in these writing activities, they expand their views about other cultures by sharing language, beliefs, religion, heritage, and their school and home life.

Teachers can also invite guest speakers available in their local area by contacting a minority community center. Speakers might be a director of an international program at a local university, a minister, or a person from the community with knowledge of a different culture. It is useful for the students to prepare questions in advance. Students should write the invitation and follow-up letter of appreciation to the speaker.

COMPETENCY 5.0 KNOWLEDGE OF ASSESSMENT OF INTEGRATED LANGUAGE ARTS

Skill 5.1   Apply results of informal assessments to instruction.

Informal assessments should be used to inform instruction. In order to make instruction more effective and to increase student learning, informal measures are best because they are more time efficient and the results are specific as to what you need to teach. Here are some examples that you might want to try.

Word Recognition: Have the student complete a self assessment that has the definitions on one side and the vocabulary words on the other. Put the vocabulary words in a box and have the student select the appropriate vocabulary to complete the sentence.

Comprehension/Study Skills: Ask student to make connections before, during, and after reading: text to self, text to text, and text to world.

Genre: Ask the student to complete a literary elements chart (includes title, author, genre (fiction or nonfiction); setting (where and when); main character(s); other character(s); plot events; climax; problem; resolution) on a book. Ask the student to list the characteristics of a specific genre or to write a short piece in that genre.

Skill 5.2   Apply results of the Florida Writing Assessment, Florida Comprehensive Assessment Test Reading, and other standardized tests to instruction.

Use of Results
Interpretations of the *FLORIDA WRITES!* achievement results are subject to several limitations. Writing achievement is limited in definition to the writing task completed during the assessment: during a 45-minute time period, students write in response to an assigned topic for the purposes of writing specified by the program without access to dictionaries or other reference materials. Because only one example of writing is collected from each student under these conditions, scores for individual students are not reliable measures of a student's general writing achievement. For each student, scores from the *FLORIDA WRITES!* must be considered in relation to how well the student writes when given a variety of classroom writing assignments.

However, the *FLORIDA WRITES!* results *will* provide a basis for identifying trends in writing over a period of several years although they do not provide an exact index of changes in performance from one year to the next year. The writing assessment employs one topic for each type of writing at each grade level. Because a topic given in any one year, by its nature, may be somewhat easier or harder for students to respond to than the topic given the previous year, differences seen in results from one year to the next are generally due to both differences in the difficulty of the topics as well as actual changes in student achievement. Performance tests like the Florida Writing Assessment that rely on the use of one topic do not lend themselves to statistical methods that can control for differences in the difficulty of the tests.

Taking into account these limitations, the results can assist in the identification of strengths and weaknesses in programs of writing instruction. Teachers and administrators may find it useful to examine the number of students scoring at different levels and the differences in student scores for each type of writing. The scores for students in a classroom or school can be interpreted in reference to sample student papers provided in the **Florida Writes!** publications for each grade level assessed and other materials available from the department. Student writing performance can be further evaluated through carefully designed classroom or school-wide writing assignments.

The **FLORIDA WRITES!** results do not represent a comprehensive evaluation of writing instruction programs. *FLORIDA WRITES!* does not measure all important aspects of writing. For example, student achievement in writing an extended manuscript or a report involving detailed information is currently not measured by *FLORIDA WRITES!* A comprehensive evaluation of student writing would take into consideration writing for a number of purposes under different conditions and would utilize information from a number of sources such as student portfolios, classroom teacher observations, and interviews with students.

Techniques critical for FCAT success include the ability to analyze, synthesize, and evaluate information. Students should practice the following activities:

Define author's purpose: to inform, to entertain, to persuade. Student activity: A title can often set the tone of the passage. Reading newspaper headings is one way to practice determining the author's purpose.

Cause and effect: Cause and effect may occur in fiction, nonfiction, poetry, and plays. Sometimes one cause will have single or multiple effects. Other times, multiple causes lead to a single effect. Creating cause and effect diagrams helps students identify these components.

Chronological order: Recognizing the order of events in a selection. A text that is chronologically organized features a sequence of events that unfold over a period of time. Student activity: read a passage to the students then complete a timeline by matching the major events to their corresponding dates.

Graphic organizers: Graphic organizers help readers think critically about an idea, concept, or story by pulling out the main idea and supporting details. These pieces of information can then be depicted graphically through the use of connected geometric shapes. Readers who develop this skill can use it to increase their reading comprehension. An example of a graphic organizer is below.

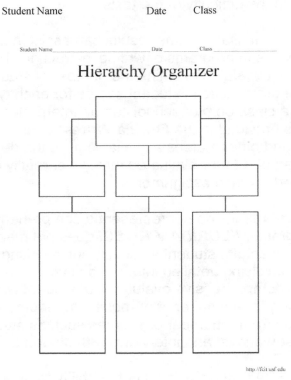

Student Name   Date   Class

Student Name_____ Date_____ Class_____

Hierarchy Organizer

http://fcit.usf.edu

Probable passage: Probable passage is a strategy to improve comprehension, develop an awareness of story structure, and increase vocabulary development. Student activity: Have a story prepared to read to the students. Then put together a chart similar to the one below. Ask the students, "Can you predict the story you will be reading? Use the vocabulary words from your story frame to complete the probable passage by placing words into the blanks."

Vocabulary:
    Zeus
    recognized
    pardoned
    arena
    forest
    bound
    freed
    capture
    lion
Setting: _____
Characters: _____
Problem: _____
Solution: _____
Ending: _____

Selective underlining: Selective underlining is an effective tool for enhancing the recall of facts. It can be used both for initial reading and response and as a reference when studying for tests. Have students identify the main idea of various short stories and articles.

Story mapping: Story mapping is a technique used after a story has been read. It includes identifying the main elements and categorizing the main events in sequential order. A graphic representation is often used to illustrate the story structure and sequence of events.

Skill 5.3   Identify appropriate and effective tools and techniques for assessing students' progress in the integrated language arts.

Academic literacy, which encompasses ways of knowing particular content and refers to strategies for understanding, discussing, organizing, and producing texts, is key to success in school. To be literate in an academic sense, one should be able to understand and to articulate conceptual relationships within, between, and among disciplines. Academic literacy also encompasses critical literacy, that is, the ability to evaluate the credibility and validity of informational sources. In a practical sense, when a student is academically literate, he/she should be able to read and understand interdisciplinary texts, to articulate comprehension through expository written pieces, and to gain further knowledge through sustained and focused research.

Developing academic literacy is especially difficult for ESL students who are struggling to acquire and improve the language and critical thinking skills they need to become full members of the academic mainstream community. The needs of these ESL students may be met through the creation of a functional language learning environment that engages them in meaningful and authentic language processing through planned, purposeful, and academically-based activities, teaching them how to extract, question, and evaluate the central points and methodology of a range of materials, and construct responses using the conventions of academic/expository writing.

Effective academic writing requires that the student be able to choose appropriate patterns of discourse, which in turn involves knowing sociolinguistic conventions relating to audience and purpose. These skills, acquired through students' attempts to process and produce texts, can be refined over time by having students complete a range of assignments of progressive complexity which derive from the sustained and focused study of one or more academic disciplines.

Sustained content area study is more effectively carried out when an extensive body of instructional and informational resources, such as is found on the internet, is available. Through its extensive collection of reading materials and numerous contexts for meaningful written communication and analysis of issues, the internet creates a highly motivating learning environment that encourages ESL students to interact with language in new and varied ways. Used as a resource for focus discipline research, the internet is highly effective in helping these students develop and refine the academic literacy so necessary for a successful educational experience.

Used as a tool for sustained content study, the internet is a powerful resource that offers easier, wider, and more rapid access to interdisciplinary information than do traditional libraries. Using the internet allows ESL students to control the direction of their reading and research, teaches them to think creatively, and increases motivation for learning as students work individually and collaboratively to gather focus discipline information. By allowing easy access to cross-referenced documents and screens, internet hypertext encourages students to read widely on interdisciplinary topics. This type of reading presents cognitively demanding language, a wide range of linguistic forms, and enables ESL students to build a wider range of schemata and a broader base of knowledge, which may help them grasp future texts. Additionally, hypermedia provides the benefit of immediate visual reinforcement through pictures and/or slideshows, facilitating comprehension of the often-abstract concepts presented in academic readings.

Academic research skills are often underdeveloped in the ESL student population making research reports especially frightening and enormously challenging. The research skills students need to complete focus discipline projects are the same skills they need to succeed in classes. Instruction that targets the development of research skills teaches ESL students the rhetorical conventions of term papers, which subsequently leads to better writing and hence improved performance in class. Moreover, the research skills acquired through sustained content study and focus discipline research enable students to manage information more effectively, which serves them throughout their academic years and into the workforce.

Conferences

An effective teacher/peer conference can be best defined as creative listening. Some characteristics of student writers that affect the conference with the teacher:

- Has little confidence that he/she has anything worth writing.
- Doesn't know where to start.
- Is sensitive to criticism.
- Wants to get the assignment done with as little effort as possible and as quickly as possible and still get an A.

Trust-building is important in teaching writing. Putting words on a page for someone else to see is an act of faith. "Touching" those words is like touching the writer's most sensitive spots. Students must believe that they will be taken seriously—that their teacher is a friend and confidant, not an enemy, and that the outcome of a writing exercise will be a pleasant experience. The teacher/student conference with writing students is very important. More will be accomplished here than in class sessions if the conference is carefully structured and carried out.

The teacher listens to what the student has come up with thus far. If the student has not managed to write anything at all, then the teacher needs to help him/her develop a strategy for moving forward. Questioning is very helpful here, remembering that the student must begin to probe his own thoughts and experiences in order to be successful in the class. There must come a time when he/she doesn't need the teacher's inquiring mind to get themes started, so the purpose of the conference is to help the student develop strategies for whatever stage of the writing process he/she is in.

If the student is clearly off on the wrong track or has not narrowed the topic sufficiently or has created a thesis that will be difficult, if not impossible, to develop, then the purpose of the conference is to help get him/her back on track and do the work on the thesis that is required, again remembering that the purpose is to help the student develop strategies for doing these things for himself/herself the next time around.

Students need as much writing practice as possible. The more times through the process, the more comfortable and accomplished they become in producing successful compositions, so as time goes on, teacher conferences should only be necessary when a student is "stuck" and needs some help getting past the blockade. In these cases, the same rules apply: creative questioning usually helps the writer move forward.

COMPETENCY 6.0 ABILITY TO WRITE WELL ON A GIVEN TOPIC

Skill 6.1   Analyze a given selection.

The first essential principle in the writing of an analysis of a literary selection is a thorough reading and understanding of the work. Once the writer feels that the author's intent is clearly understood, the thesis statement of the analysis must be determined. It will probably be a declaration of the purpose of the author in the work, itself. For example, if one were analyzing Mitch Albom's *The Five People You Meet in Heaven*, the thesis for the analysis might be as follows: "The theme of this story is that living to serve others gives meaning to the end of one's life."

However, the writer can make a point that is meaningful by focusing on other aspects of the story. For example, the *style* of a writer like Ernest Hemingway is so unusual and significant that the thesis might focus on that aspect of one of his stories. Setting may play a special role in a story and might make a good thesis for analysis. In fact, any aspect of the story can be useful for this kind of paper. This choice is important and will drive how the analysis is developed.

Once the thesis is decided, the next steps just naturally fall in line. The first step is a search for passages that support or relate to the theme idea. Even before the thesis has been decided upon, the writer should have been taking notes, possibly on the pages of the book itself. Once the thesis is determined, then he/she will go back through the work, looking at the notes already made but adding or adjusting them to make sure adequate material is available to support the thesis of the analysis. By this time, the notes should begin to be recorded on a sheet of paper or in the word processor. Specifics are important here as are details if the analysis is to be complete and effective. In this second reading, the thesis might change—either to an entirely different one or to a variation of the first one.

It's not enough to just present illustrative material; it must be organized in such a way that it is logical and reasonable to the reader of the analysis. In other words, a preliminary outline of the final paper should be determined here. The steps may be in a different order than the illustrations appear in the work itself. One from later in the book might be relevant to an earlier one. The earlier one might foreshadow a later one, for instance.

In referring to a work of fiction, the record should always be in the present tense. For example, instead of Eddie *worked* in a maintenance shop—spreading grease, tightening bolts, etc., it should be: Eddie works in a maintenance shop—spreading grease, tightening bolts, etc. Keeping the tenses in the present requires special care. This is a good exercise in verb tenses for students.

It should be remembered that this is a recursive process. Nothing is set in stone until the paper is ready to be handed in. Things will be seen on the second and third readings that were not apparent the first time through, and the writer must feel free to make changes that make the point clearer or stronger. Even the thesis or the aspect of the story that will be the focus of the analysis is open to change until the last stage of the writing process. Students sometimes have difficulty coming to a decision, so they should be encouraged to set time limits on themselves for making the decisions and completing the various steps required to write a successful paper.

Helping students become successful writers of literary analyses depends on several factors. They should have plenty of experience in analysis in class. The short story is a good way to help students develop the confidence that they can do this kind of writing, which requires independent reasoning. Using the short story as the basis for a writing course gives students more opportunities to go through the analyzing process and gives them more opportunities to practice their analytical skills. The role of the teacher is to continually teach the principles but also to encourage independent thinking in these matters, even to accept sometimes less-than-perfect analyses.

Ultimately, the analysis should be the convictions arrived upon as a result of the reading and understanding the text. This is a good opportunity to help students begin to take responsibility for what they write—an important objective for a writing course.

Skill 6.2   Organize ideas around a focal point.

Techniques to Maintain Focus:
- **Focus on a main point.** The point should be clear to readers, and all sentences in the paragraph should relate to it.
- **Start the paragraph with a topic sentence.** This should be a general, one-sentence summary of the paragraph's main point, relating both back toward the thesis and toward the content of the paragraph. (A topic sentence is sometimes unnecessary if the paragraph continues a developing idea clearly introduced in a preceding paragraph, or if the paragraph appears in a narrative of events where generalizations might interrupt the flow of the story.)
- **Stick to the point.** Eliminate sentences that do not support the topic sentence.

Be flexible. If there is not enough evidence to support the claim your topic sentence is making, do not fall into the trap of wandering or introducing new ideas within the paragraph. Either find more evidence, or adjust the topic sentence to match the evidence that is available.

Prior to writing, you will need to prewrite for ideas and details as well as decide how the essay will be organized. In the hour you have to write you should spend no more than 5-10 minutes prewriting and organizing your ideas. As you prewrite, it might be helpful to remember you should have at least three main points and at least two to three details to support your main ideas. There are several types of graphic organizers that you should practice using as you prepare for the essay portion of the test.

PRACTICE - Choose one topic from the chart on page and complete the cluster.

PREWRITE TO EXPLAIN HOW OR WHY

Reread a question from the chart on the previous page that asks you to explain how a poet creates tone and mood using imagery and word choice. Then fill out the organizer on the following page that identifies how the poet effectively creates tone and mood. Support with examples from the poem.

VISUAL ORGANIZER: GIVING REASONS

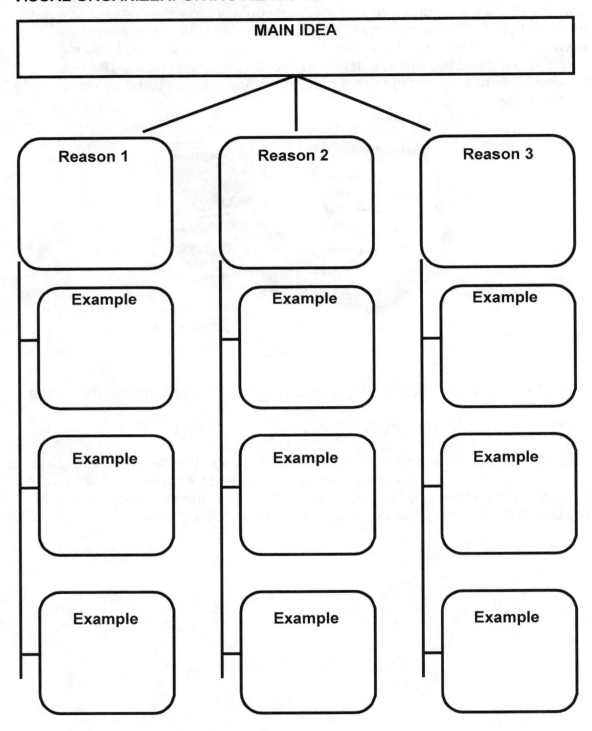

STEP 3: PREWRITE TO ORGANIZE IDEAS

After you have completed a graphic organizer, you need to decide how you will organize your essay. To organize your essay, you might consider one of the following patterns:.

1. Examine individual elements such as **plot**, **setting**, **theme**, **character**, **point of view**, **tone**, **mood**, or **style**.

   SINGLE ELEMENT OUTLINE
   Intro - main idea statement
   Main point 1 with at least two supporting details
   Main point 2 with at least two supporting details
   Main point 3 with at least two supporting details
   Conclusion (restates main ideas and summary of main pts)

2. **Compare and contrast two elements.**

POINT-BY-POINT	BLOCK
Introduction Statement of main idea about A and B	Introduction Statement of main idea about A and B
Main Point 1 Discussion of A Discussion of B	Discussion of A Main Point 1 Main Point 2 Main point 3
Main Point 2 Discussion of A Discussion of B	Discussion of B Main Point 1 Main Point 2 Main Point 3
Main Point 3 Discussion of A Discussion of B	Conclusion Restate main idea
Conclusion Restatement or summary of main idea	

PRACTICE:
Using the cluster on the next page, choose an organizing chart and complete for your topic.

VISUAL ORGANIZER: GIVING INFORMATION

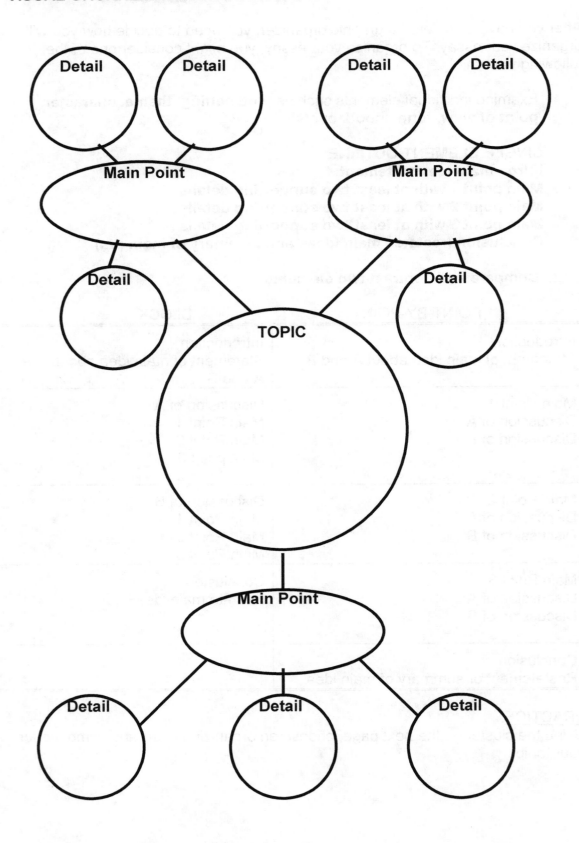

Skill 6.3   Incorporate appropriate elements of style to enhance readers' interest and understanding.

Introductions:

It's important to remember that in the writing process, the introduction should be written last. Until the body of the paper has been determined—thesis, development—it's difficult to make strategic decisions regarding the introduction. The Greek rhetoricians called this part of a discourse *exordium*, a "leading into." The basic purpose of the introduction, then, is to lead the audience into the discourse. It can let the reader know what the purpose of the discourse is and it can condition the audience to be receptive to what the writer wants to say. It can be very brief or it can take up a large percentage of the total word count. Aristotle said that the introduction could be compared to the flourishes that flute players make before their performance—an overture in which the musicians display what they can play best in order to gain the favor and attention of the audience for the main performance.

In order to do this, we must first of all know what we are going to say; who the readership is likely to be; what the social, political, economic, etc., climate is; what preconceived notions the audience is likely to have regarding the subject; and how long the discourse is going to be.

There are many ways to do this:
- Show that the subject is important.
- Show that although the points we are presenting may seem improbable, they are true.
- Show that the subject has been neglected, misunderstood, or misrepresented.
- Explain an unusual mode of development.
- Forestall any misconception of the purpose.
- Apologize for a deficiency.
- Arouse interest in the subject with an anecdotal lead-in.
- Ingratiate oneself with the readership.
- Establish one's own credibility.

The introduction often ends with the thesis, the point or purpose of the paper. However, this is not set in stone. The thesis may open the body of the discussion, or it may conclude the discourse. The most important thing to remember is that the purpose and structure of the introduction should be deliberate if it is to serve the purpose of "leading the reader into the discussion."

Conclusions:

It's easier to write a conclusion after the decisions regarding the introduction have been made. Aristotle taught that the conclusion should strive to do five things:

1. Inspire the reader with a favorable opinion of the writer.
2. Amplify the force of the points made in the body of the paper.
3. Reinforce the points made in the body.
4. Rouse appropriate emotions in the reader.
5. Restate in a summary way what has been said.

The conclusion may be short or it may be long depending on its purpose in the paper. Recapitulation, a brief restatement of the main points or certainly of the thesis is the most common form of effective conclusions. A good example is the closing argument in a court trial.

Text Organization:

In studies of professional writers and how they produce their successful works, it has been revealed that writing is a process that can be clearly defined although in practice it must have enough flexibility to allow for creativity. The teacher must be able to define the various stages that a successful writer goes through in order to make a statement that has value. There must be a discovery stage when ideas, materials, supporting details, etc., are deliberately collected. These may come from many possible sources: the writer's own experience and observations, deliberate research of written sources, interviews of live persons, television presentations, or the internet.

The next stage is organization where the purpose, thesis, and supporting points are determined. Most writers will put forth more than one possible thesis and in the next stage, the writing of the paper, settle on one as the result of trial and error. Once the paper is written, the editing stage is necessary and is probably the most important stage. This is not just the polishing stage. At this point, decisions must be made regarding whether the reasoning is cohesive—does it hold together? Is the arrangement the best possible one or should the points be rearranged? Are there holes that need to be filled in? What form will the introduction take? Does the conclusion lead the reader out of the discourse or is it inadequate or too abrupt, etc.

It's important to remember that the best writers engage in all of these stages recursively. They may go back to discovery at any point in the process. They may go back and rethink the organization, etc. To help students become effective writers, the teacher needs to give them adequate practice in the various stages and encourage them to engage deliberately in the creative thinking that makes writers successful.

Enhancing Interest:

- Start out with an attention-grabbing introduction. This sets an engaging tone for the entire piece and will be more likely to pull the reader in.
- Use dynamic vocabulary and varied sentence beginnings. Keep the readers on their toes. If they can predict what you are going to say next, switch it up.
- Avoid using clichés (as cold as ice, the best thing since sliced bread, nip it in the bud). These are easy shortcuts, but they are not interesting, memorable, or convincing.

Ensuring Understanding:

- Avoid using the words, "clearly," "obviously," and "undoubtedly." Often, things that are clear or obvious to the author are not as apparent to the reader. Instead of using these words, make your point so strongly that it is clear on its own.
- Use the word that best fits the meaning you intend, even if it is longer or a little less common. Try to find a balance; go with a familiar yet precise word.
- When in doubt, explain further.

Skill 6.4   Incorporate relevant content, using ample supporting details from the selection.

Once a topic has been selected, for example, "Immigration," then the search for resources begins. This topic, like many, has so much information available that a review of titles will suggest ways to narrow it, the next step in the process. If the topic is narrowed to "Protecting our southern border," then some of the better, more interesting ones can be selected. Some will be hard-copy—newspapers, journals, etc.,—and some will be electronic, found on the Internet.

Everything that will be used must be documented. Don't fail to gather and organize bibliographic information at the very outset. To fail to do this leads to frustration and lost time. Also, everything that will be used must be read thoroughly if it's to be useful. While reading, underlining, highlighting, or taking notes is advised. On hard copy, if you don't own the copy and are unable to underline or highlight, you might consider Xeroxing it so you can do so. Otherwise, you'll need to settle for note-taking. This can be done with note pad and pencil or it can be done in a word-processed document as you go. Be sure to identify all the notes as you go. If you are taking notes from an electronic document, you can copy it into Word and use the highlighter or simply take notes, again being sure to put in identifiers as you go.

Now you are ready to organize your paper. Just as with any other piece of writing, this paper should have a thesis. What idea are you going to support with the information you've found? If you've decided, for instance, on "Putting up a high fence is the best way to deal with the immigrant problem," you will use the information taken from your sources to support that. Some of the information may be used to show the arguments against your thesis, so you can borrow from the documents that support it to refute the opposing point of view. Remember, you will probably need to discard some of the material, even though you may have spent time on it. You don't want irrelevancies in your final document.

The ideas taken from other people must be identified. It can be as simple as "John Jones, a Texas legislator feels . . ." or it can be footnoted or end noted. The role of the transitional paragraph is important in a synthesis of what others are saying. In the editing stage of this paper, you will want to ask yourself whether enough has been done to move from one point to the next, whether there are abrupt shifts that are confusing, and whether you may need to insert some transitional paragraphs in certain places.

The essay will end with a concluding paragraph that will draw everything together and restate the thesis.

The old adage that a picture is worth a thousand words is never more evident than in the use of charts, graphs, and tables to make a point clear. It's one thing to say that the GDP of the United States rose fifteen percentage points in the last five years, it's an entirely different thing to show a graph that depicts that rapid rise. If the point being made is that the increase in the GDP is better than it has ever been in the past fifty years, then a graph showing that growth cinches the point. If the point being made is that the growth in the GDP corresponds to the growth of the stock market for the same period, then that also can be graphed.

It's important that data in charts and graphs be simple and comprehensive. Also, it should only be used if it does, in fact, display the information more effectively than words alone can. However, it should also be able to stand alone. It should make the point by itself. If two or more charts or tables are used within a work, they should be consistent in style. Whatever graphic is used, elements of the same kind must always be represented in the same way. This is not a time to be artistic graphically; visual effects should be used only for the purpose of making the point, not for variety.

In graphs, both the horizontal and vertical axes should be labeled. In a column, both column heads and stubs should be labeled. In a graph, the vertical axis is always read from the bottom up and curves or bars should be graphically distinct (color or dotted lines, for example) and all elements should be clearly identified in a key. The title appears in a caption rather than as a title and is lowercased except for names that would normally be capitalized in the text. If abbreviations are used, care should be taken to make them easily recognizable unless they are explained in the key or in the caption.

A table can often give information that would take several paragraphs to present and can do so more clearly. Tables should be as simple as the material allows and should be understandable without explanation even to a reader who might be unfamiliar with the subject matter. Only necessary explanations should be presented in the text; the table should be able to stand alone.

The advent of word processing makes the creation and insertion of charts, graphs, and tables much more practical than ever before.

It takes very little knowledge or skill to create these illustrative devices, and helping students develop those skills is a valuable enhancement to a writing course.

Skill 6.5 Apply conventions of standard English.

While it's very difficult to define exactly what Standard English is, for the English teacher, it's important to settle on a definition that is practicable in the classes that attempt to teach or promote it. Since English has become the closest to a universal language that any language has ever attained because of its use in international business and tourism, it also has many more dialects than most languages. Classrooms in California are usually filled with speakers of a variety of these dialects, which presents a special challenge for the teacher of English.

It's important to remember that language is very personal. Requiring students from Hispanic families and communities to abandon their own dialect and replace it with the "standard" one may suggest to them that they or their families and communities are personally sub-standard. They will be resistant to accepting the new dialect and will probably resent the implication that they are inherently inferior to other students. There are many sensitive ways to deal with this situation, and teaching about dialects before any attempt is made to teach "standard English" is a good way to go. Respect for all dialects on the part of the teacher is important. Many of the variations in the speech of ghettoized African-Americans are in many ways more efficient in making a point clear and in descriptive elegance than the standard dialect. Studying important writers such as Oscar Hijuelos and Maya Angelou who have used those features of the dialect in special and endearing ways can be useful in helping students understand how effective dialectal differences can be. This is also a good time to teach the use of dictionaries and encyclopedias to help writers and speakers use words in a way that will be understood by all listeners.

Perhaps the best definition of Standard English is that it is the dialect spoken by successful radio and television announcers and newspeople. To succeed in the public arena, speakers and writers need to be understood by the greatest number of people possible. It is also the dialect of the business world. If a student aspires to succeed in a business environment, knowing Standard English is an important building block for success. In addition, it is the dialect used in most written communications. If a newspaper article were written in a Hispanic dialect of English, many people would not understand it. However, if it is written in Standard English, even the speakers of that dialect will understand it. If a legal brief were written in African-American dialect, it would not make it into the courtroom. Again, if it were written in Standard English, everyone involved, even native speakers of the African-American dialect will understand it.

So what exactly is Standard English? It is the dialect of the English handbook or textbook that forms the basis for the English classroom curriculum. It is also the dialect of dictionaries and encyclopedias. Guiding students through the English texts and handbooks is a method of teaching Standard English. Marking student papers on the foundation established in the lessons from the textbooks and handbooks is an exercise in teaching Standard English.

Sample Test

<u>**Essay Question**</u>

Read the passage below from *The Diary of Anne Frank* (1947); then complete the exercise that follows.

Written on July 15, 1944, three weeks before the Frank family was arrested by the Nazis, Anne's diary entry explains her worldview and future hopes.

"It's difficult in times like these: ideals, dreams and cherished hopes rise within us, only to be crushed by grim reality. It's a wonder I haven't abandoned all my ideals, they seem so absurd and impractical. Yet I cling to them because I still believe, in spite of everything, that people are truly good at heart.

"It's utterly impossible for me to build my life on a foundation of chaos, suffering and death. I see the world being slowly transformed into a wilderness, I hear the approaching thunder that, one day, will destroy us too, I feel the suffering of millions, And yet, when I look up at the sky, I somehow feel that everything will change for the better, that this cruelty too shall end, that peace and tranquility will return once more. In the meantime, I must hold on to my ideals. Perhaps the day will come when I will be able to realize them!"

Using your knowledge of literature, write a response in which you:

- Compare and contrast Anne's ideals with her awareness of the conditions in which she lives; and
- Discuss how the structure of Anne's writing—her sentences and paragraphs—emphasize the above contrast.

Sample Weak Response

Anne Frank's ideals in this writing make readers clear on the point that she was strongly against Hitler and the Nazis. You can tell that she knows the Nazis are very dangerous and violent people who cause "the suffering of millions." Otherwise, why would she have written this? This fact of Nazis causing the suffering of millions of people, and killing them, is a large contrast to how much she believes "that people are truly good at heart." Anne Frank is right about her ideals. And that is why her whole book is such a large contrast to the conditions in which she lived in WWII, when everything was going wrong in the world. You can also tell from this passage that she is a lot smarter than Hitler was. That is another big contrast in the book.

Anne's sentences and paragraphs emphasize the above contrast. They are not fiction; they are her own real thoughts, and these thoughts don't cause "a grim reality" of "cruelty" or the "absurd and impractical" things that she talks about as the war's fault. No, Anne's words cause us to see what is true and real in her art and in her heart. She makes us see that love is not the fiction. Hitler and the Nazis are the ones who make the fiction. We can read this in between the lines, which sometimes has to be done.

Back when Anne Frank wrote her words down on paper, everything was going wrong around her but she knew what to do, and she did it. She wrote a world classic story about her life. This story is a big contrast to what the Germans were doing.

Sample Strong Response

This excerpt from *The Diary of Anne Frank* reveals the inner strength of a young girl who refuses, despite the wartime violence and danger surrounding her, to let her idealism be overcome by hatred and mass killing. This idealism is reflected, in part, by her emphases on universal human hopes such as peace, tranquility, and goodwill. But Anne Frank is no dreamy Pollyanna. Reflecting on her idealism in the context of the war raging around her, she matter-of-factly writes: "my dreams, they seem so absurd and impractical."

This indicates Anne Frank's awareness of not only her own predicament but of human miseries that extend beyond the immediate circumstances of her life. For elsewhere she writes in a similar vein, "In times like these… I see the world being slowly transformed into a wilderness"; despite her own suffering she can "feel the suffering of millions."

And yet Anne Frank believes, "in spite of everything, that people are truly good at heart." This statement epitomizes the stark existential contrast of her worldview with the wartime reality that ultimately claimed her life.

The statement also exemplifies how Anne's literary form—her syntax and diction—mirror thematic content and contrasts. "In spite of everything," she still believes in people. She can "hear the approaching thunder…yet, when I look up at the sky, I somehow feel that everything will change for the better." At numerous points in this diary entry, first-hand knowledge of violent tragedy stands side-by-side with belief in humanity and human progress.

"I must hold on to my ideals," Anne concludes. "Perhaps the day will come when I'll be able to realize them!" In her diary she has done so, and more.

Multiple Choice

Choose the best answer for each of the questions.

1. After watching a movie of a train derailment, a child exclaims, "Wow, look how many cars fell off the tracks. There's junk everywhere. The engineer must have really been asleep." Using the facts that the child is impressed by the wreckage and assigns blame to the engineer, a follower of Piaget's theories would estimate the child to be about:
(*Rigorous*)(*Skill 1.1*)

   A. ten years old
   B. twelve years old
   C. fourteen years old
   D. sixteen years old

2. Children's literature became established in the:
(*Rigorous*)(*Skill 1.1*)

   A. seventeenth century
   B. eighteenth century
   C. nineteenth century
   D. twentieth century

3. In the hierarchy of needs for adolescents who are becoming more team-oriented in their approach to learning, which need do they exhibit most?
(*Average Rigor*)(*Skill1.1*)

   A. Need for competence
   B. Need for love/acceptance
   C. Need to know
   D. Need to belong

4. Which aspect of language is innate?
(*Rigorous*)(*Skill 2.1*)

   A. Biological capability to articulate sounds understood by other humans
   B. Cognitive ability to create syntactical structures
   C. Capacity for using semantics to convey meaning in a social environment
   D. Ability to vary inflections and accents

5. **The most significant drawback to applying learning theory research to classroom practice is that:** *(Rigorous)(Skill2.2)*

   A. today's students do not acquire reading skills with the same alacrity as when greater emphasis was placed on reading classical literature
   B. development rates are complicated by geographical and cultural differences that are difficult to overcome
   C. homogeneous grouping has contributed to faster development of some age groups
   D. social and environmental conditions have contributed to an escalated maturity level than research done twenty or more years ago would seem to indicate

6. **Computer-assisted instruction (CAI) accommodates all of the following factors in reading instruction _except for:_** *(Average Rigor)(Skill 2.5)*

   A. free-form responses to comprehension questions
   B. increased motivation
   C. the addition of speech with computer-presented text
   D. the use of computers for word processing, and the integration of writing instruction with reading

7. **To explain or to inform belongs in the category of** *(Average Rigor)(Skill 3.1)*

   A. exposition.
   B. narration.
   C. persuasion.
   D. description.

8. **Modeling is a practice that requires students to:** *(Rigorous)(Skill 3.1)*

   A. create a style unique to their own language capabilities
   B. emulate the writing of professionals
   C. paraphrase passages from good literature
   D. peer evaluate the writings of other students.

9. **Which level of meaning is the hardest aspect of a language to master?** *(Rigorous)(Skill 3.2)*

   A. denotation
   B. jargon
   C. connotation
   D. slang

10. **Which of the following terms does _not_ denote a figure of speech (figurative language)?** *(Rigorous)(Skill 3.2)*

    A. Simile
    B. Euphemism
    C. Onomatopoeia
    D. Allusion

11. The appearance of a Yankee from Connecticut in the Court of King Arthur is an example of a/an:
(Rigorous)(Skill3.2)

A. rhetoric
B. parody
C. paradox
D. anachronism

12. This statement, "I'll die if I don't pass this course," exemplifies a/an:
(Average Rigor)(Skill 3.2)

A. barbarism
B. oxymoron
C. hyperbole
D. antithesis

13. A figure of speech in which someone absent or something inhuman is addressed as though present and able to respond describes:
(Average Rigor)(Skill 3.2)

A. personification
B. synecdoche
C. metonymy
D. apostrophe

14. *Diction* is best defined as:
(Average Rigor)(Skill 3.2)

A. the specific word choices an author makes in order to create a particular mood or feeling in the reader
B. writing that explains something thoroughly
C. the background, or exposition, for a short story or drama
D. word choices that help teach a truth or moral

15. The literary device of personification is used in which example below?
(Easy)(Skill3.2)

A. "Beg me no beggary by soul or parents, whining dog!"
B. "Happiness sped through the halls cajoling as it went."
C. "O wind thy horn, thou proud fellow."
D. "And that one talent which is death to hide."

16. **Read the following passage:**

    "It would have been hard to find a passer-by more wretched in appearance. He was a man of middle height, stout and hardy, in the strength of maturity; he might have been forty-six or seven. A slouched leather cap hid half his face, bronzed by the sun and wind, and dripping with sweat."

    What is its main form of discourse?(*Easy*)(*Skill3.2*)

    A. Description
    B. Narration
    C. Exposition
    D. Persuasion

17. **A paper written in first person and having characters, a setting, a plot, some dialogue, and events sequenced chronologically with some flashbacks exemplifies which genre? (*Easy*) (*Skill 3.2*)**

    A. Exposition
    B. Narration
    C. Persuasion
    D. Speculation

18. **"Clean as a whistle" and "easy as falling off a log" exemplify:**
    (*Easy*)(*Skill 3.2*)

    A. semantics
    B. parody
    C. irony
    D. clichés

19. **Middle school students bring little, if any, initial experience in**
    (*Rigorous*)(*Skill 3.3*)

    A. phonics
    B. phonemics
    C. textbook reading assignments
    D. stories read by the teacher

20. **Regularly requiring students to practice reading short, instructional-level texts at least three times to a peer and to give and receive peer feedback about these readings mainly addresses which reading skill? (*Average Rigor*)(*Skill 3.6*)**

    A. Comprehension
    B. Fluency
    C. Evaluation
    D. Word-solving

21. Before reading a passage, a teacher gives her students an anticipation guide with a list of statements related to the topic they are about to cover in the reading material. She asks the students to indicate their agreement or disagreement with each statement on the guide. This activity is intended to *(Average Rigor)(Skill 3.6)*

A. elicit students' prior knowledge of the topic and set a purpose for reading
B. help students to identify the main ideas and supporting details in the text
C. help students to synthesize information from the text
D. help students to visualize the concepts and terms in the text

22. A conversation between two or more people is called a/an: *(Easy) (Skill 4.3)*

A. parody
B. dialogue
C. monologue
D. analogy

23. Among junior-high school students of low-to-average readability levels, which work would most likely stir reading interest? *(Average Rigor)(Skill4.3)*

A. *Elmer Gantry*, Sinclair Lewis
B. *Smiley's People*, John Le Carre
C. *The Outsiders*, S.E. Hinton
D. *And Then There Were None*, Agatha Christie.

24. Consider the following poem:

My name is John Welington Wells,
I'm a dealer in magic and spells,
In blessings and curses,
And ever-fill'd purses,
In prophecies, witches, and knells.

This poem would be considered a: *(Average Rigor)(Skill 4.3)*

A. sonnet
B. haiku
C. limerick
D. cinquain

25. Which of the following would be the most significant factor in teaching Homer's *Iliad* and *Odyssey* to any particular group of students? *(Rigorous)(Skill4.3)*

    A. Identifying a translation on the appropriate reading level
    B. Determining the student's interest level
    C. Selecting an appropriate evaluative technique
    D. Determining the scope and delivery methods of background study

26. If a student uses slang and expletives, what is the best course of action to take in order to improve the student's formal communication skills? *(Easy)(Skill 4.4)*

    A. Ask the student to rephrase their writing; that is, translate it into language appropriate for the school principal to read
    B. Refuse to read the student's papers until he conforms to a more literate style
    C. Ask the student to read his work aloud to the class for peer evaluation
    D. Rewrite the flagrant passages to show the student the right form of expression

27. Oral debate is most closely associated with which form of discourse? *(Easy)(Skill 4.4)*

    A. Description
    B. Exposition
    C. Narration
    D. Persuasion

28. The substitution of "went to his rest" for "died" exemplifies a/an: *(Easy)(Skill 4.4)*

    A. bowdlerism
    B. jargon
    C. euphemism
    D. malapropism

29. The students in Mrs. Cline's seventh grade language arts class were invited to attend a performance of *Romeo and Juliet* presented by the drama class at the high school. To best prepare, they should: *(Rigorous) (Skill 4.4)*

    A. read the play as a homework exercise
    B. read a synopsis of the plot and a biographical sketch of the author
    C. examine a few main selections from the play to become familiar with the language and style of the author
    D. read a condensed version of the story and practice attentive listening skills

30. Which of the following is the least effective procedure for promoting consciousness of audience? *(Rigorous)(Skill 4.7)*

    A. Pairing students during the writing process
    B. Reading all rough drafts before the students write the final copies
    C. Having students compose stories or articles for publication in school literary magazines or newspapers
    D. Writing letters to friends or relatives

31. A student informative composition should consist of a minimum of how many paragraphs? *(Average Rigor)(Skill 4.7)*

    A. Three
    B. Four
    C. Five
    D. Six

32. In 'inverted triangle' introductory paragraphs, the thesis sentence occurs: *(Average Rigor)(Skill 4.7)*

    A. at the beginning of the paragraph
    B. in the middle of the paragraph
    C. at the end of the paragraph
    D. in the second paragraph

33. A punctuation mark indicating omission, interrupted thought, or an incomplete statement is a/an: *(Easy) (Skill 4.8)*

    A. ellipsis
    B. anachronism
    C. colloquy
    D. idiom

34. Which of the four underlined sections of the following sentence contains an error that a word processing spellchecker probably wouldn't catch? *(Easy)(Skill 4.8)*

    He tuc the hors by the rains and pulled it back to the stabel.

    A. tuc
    B. hors
    C. rains
    D. stabel

35. For students with poor vocabularies, the teacher should recommend first that: *(Easy) (Skill 4.8)*

    A. they enroll in a Latin class
    B. they read newspapers, magazines, and books on a regular basis
    C. they write the words repetitively after looking them up in the dictionary
    D. they use a thesaurus to locate and incorporate the synonyms found there into their vocabularies

36. **Which group of words is not a sentence?** *(Easy)(Skill 4.8)*

    A. In keeping with the graduation tradition, the students, in spite of the rain, standing in the cafeteria tossing their mortarboards.
    B. Rosa Parks, who refused to give up her seat on the bus, will be forever remembered for her courage.
    C. Taking advantage of the goalie's being out of the net, we scored our last and winning goal.
    D. When it began to rain, we gathered our possessions and ran for the pavilion.

37. **The arrangement and relationship of words in sentences or sentence structures best describes:** *(Average Rigor) (Skill 4.8)*

    A. style
    B. discourse
    C. thesis
    D. syntax

38. **Identify the sentence that has an error in parallel structure.** *(Average Rigor)(Skill 4.8)*

    A. In order to help your favorite cause, you should contribute time or money, raise awareness, and write congressmen.
    B. Many people envision scientists working alone in a laboratory and discovering scientific breakthroughs.
    C. Some students prefer watching videos to textbooks because they are used for visual presentation.
    D. Tom Hanks, who has won two Academy Awards, is celebrated as an actor, director, and producer.

39. **Consider the following sentence:**

    Joe ***didn't hardly know his cousin Fred***, *who'd had a rhinoplasty*.

    Which word group below best conveys the intended meaning of the underlined section above? *(Average Rigor)(Skill 4.8)*

    A. hardly did know his cousin Fred
    B. didn't know his cousin Fred hardly
    C. hardly knew his cousin Fred
    D. didn't know his cousin Fred

40. **Which of the following bits of information best describes the structure of English?** *(Average Rigor)(Skill 4.8)*

    A. Syntax based on word order
    B. Inflected
    C. Romantic
    D. Orthography is phonetic

41. **Use the table below to answer the question that follows it.**

	Math Usage	General Usage
bi (two)	bilinear	bicycle
	bimodal	biplane
	binomial	bifocals
cent (100)	centimeter	century
	centigram	centigrade
	percent	centipede
circum (around)	circumference	circumnavigate
	circumradius	circumstance
	circumcenter	Circumspect

    Which vocabulary strategy does the table above exemplify? *(Rigorous)(Skill4.8)*

    A. Frayer method
    B. Morphemic analysis
    C. Semantic mapping
    D. Word mapping

42. **Which of the following contains an error in possessive punctuation?** *(Rigorous)(Skill 4.8)*

    A. Doris's shawl
    B. mother's-in-law frown
    C. children's lunches
    D. ambassador's briefcase

43. **Which of the following sentences is unambiguously properly punctuated?** *(Rigorous)(Skill 4.8)*

    A. The more you eat; the more you want.
    B. The authors—John Steinbeck, Ernest Hemingway, and William Faulkner—are staples of modern writing in American literature textbooks.
    C. Handling a wild horse, takes a great deal of skill and patience
    D. The man, who replaced our teacher, is a comedian.

44. **Consider the following sentence:**

    Mr. Brown is a school volunteer __with a reputation and twenty years service__.

    Which phrase below best represents the logical intent of the underlined phrase above? *(Rigorous)(Skill 4.8)*

    A. with a reputation for twenty years' service
    B. with a reputation for twenty year's service
    C. who has served twenty years
    D. with a service reputation of twenty years

45. **Which of the following sentences contains an error in agreement?** *(Rigorous)(Skill 4.8)*

   A. Jennifer is one of the women who writes for the magazine.
   B. Each one of their sons plays a different sport.
   C. This band has performed at the Odeum many times.
   D. The data are available online at the listed website.

46. **Which item below is not a research-based strategy that supports reading?** *(Rigorous)(Skill 4.9)*

   A. Reading more
   B. Reading along with a more proficient reader
   C. Reading a passage no more than twice
   D. Self-monitoring progress

47. **All of the following techniques are used to conduct ongoing informal assessment of student progress *except for:*** *(Rigorous) (Skill 5.1)*

   A. analyzing the student work product at key stages
   B. collecting data from assessment tests
   C. posing strategic questions
   D. observing students as they work

48. **A formative evaluation of student writing:** *(Rigorous) (Skill 5.1)*

   A. requires a thorough marking of mechanical errors with a pencil or pen
   B. makes comments on the appropriateness of the student's interpretation of the prompt and the degree to which the objective was met
   C. requires the student to hand in all the materials produced during the process of writing
   D. involves several careful readings of the text for content, mechanics, spelling, and usage

49. **Effective assessment requires that:** *(Average Rigor) (Skill 5.1)*

   A. students not be involved in the assessment process
   B. testing activities are kept separate from the teaching activities
   C. references materials that classroom instruction has prepared the students to read
   D. tests, in order to be reliable, should never use materials previously studied in the classroom

50. **Effective assessment means that:** *(Easy) (Skill 5.2)*

   A. it ignores age and cultural considerations
   B. students' weaknesses are emphasized
   C. only reading skills count
   D. it is integrated with instruction and is not intrusive

51. **A paper explaining the relationship between food and weight gain contains the signal words "because," "consequently," "this is how," and "due to." These words suggest that the paper has which text structure?** *(Easy)(Skill 5.2)*

   A. Cause and effect structure
   B. Compare and contrast structure
   C. Descriptive structure
   D. Sequential structure

52. **To enhance reading comprehension, experts recommend all of these techniques _except for_:** *(Average Rigor) (Skill 5.2)*

   A. reading material through only once, but read slowly and carefully
   B. reading material through more than once according to a plan
   C. creating a map for the next reading
   D. highlighting or taking notes during reading

53. **A composition with no voice will lack the following quality** *(Rigorous) (Skill 5.2)*

   A. organization
   B. appeal
   C. illustrations
   D. ideas

54. **Varying the complexity of a graphic organizer exemplifies differentiating which aspect of a lesson?** *(Rigorous)(Skill 5.2)*

   A. Its content/topic
   B. Its environment
   C. Its process
   D. Its product

55. **A teacher has taught his students to self-monitor their reading by locating where in the passage they are having difficulty, by identifying the specific problem there, and by restating the difficult sentence or passage in their own words. These strategies are examples of:** *(Rigorous) (Skill 5.2)*

   A. graphic and semantic organizers
   B. metacognition
   C. recognizing story structure
   D. summarizing

56. **Reading assessment should take place:** *(Average Rigor) (Skill 5.3)*

   A. at the end of the semester
   B. at the end of a unit
   C. constantly
   D. all of the above

57. Overcrowded classes prevent the individual attention needed to facilitate language development. This drawback can be best overcome by *(Average Rigor) (Skill 5.3)*

   A. dividing the class into independent study groups
   B. assigning more study time at home
   C. using more drill practice in class
   D. team teaching

58. Which of the following is not true about English? *(Easy)(Skill 5.3)*

   A. English is the easiest language to learn
   B. English is the least inflected language
   C. English has the most extensive vocabulary of any language
   D. English originated as a Germanic tongue

59. Which of the following responses to literature typically give middle school students the most problems? *(Rigorous)(Skill 6.1)*

   A. Interpretive
   B. Evaluative
   C. Critical
   D. Emotional

60. Writing ideas quickly without interruption of the flow of thoughts or attention to conventions is called: *(Average Rigor) (Skill 6.2)*

   A. brainstorming
   B. mapping
   C. listing
   D. free writing

61. In a timed essay test of an hour's duration, how much time should be devoted to prewriting?*(Rigorous)(Skill 6.2)*

   A. Five minutes
   B. Ten minutes
   C. Fifteen minutes
   D. Twenty minutes

62. Which of the following is not a technique of prewriting? *(Average Rigor)(Skill 6.2)*

   A. Clustering
   B. Listing
   C. Brainstorming
   D. Proofreading

63. Reading a piece of student writing to assess the overall impression of the product is *(Average Rigor) (Skill 6.2)*

   A. holistic evaluation.
   B. portfolio assessment.
   C. analytical evaluation.
   D. using a performance system.

64. **Which of the following should not be included in the opening paragraph of an informative essay? (Average Rigor)(Skill 6.3)**

    A. Thesis sentence
    B. Details and examples supporting the main idea
    C. Broad general introduction to the topic
    D. A style and tone that grabs the reader's attention

Answer Key

1. A		45. A	
2. A		46. C	
3. B		47. B	
4. A		48. B	
5. D		49. C	
6. A		50. D	
7. A		51. A	
8. B		52. A	
9. C		53. B	
10. D		54. C	
11. D		55. C	
12. C		56. D	
13. D		57. A	
14. A		58. A	
15. B		59. B	
16. A		60. D	
17. B		61. B	
18. D		62. D	
19. C		63. A	
20. B		64. B	
21. A			
22. B			
23. C			
24. C			
25. A			
26. A			
27. D			
28. C			
29. D			
30. B			
31. C			
32. C			
33. A			
34. C			
35. B			
36. A			
37. D			
38. C			
39. C			
40. A			
41. B			
42. B			
43. B			
44. D			

Rigor Table

	Easy %20	Average Rigor %40	Rigorous %40
Question #	16, 17, 18, 19, 23, 27, 28, 29, 34, 35, 36, 37, 51, 52 , 61	6, 7,12, 13, 14, 15, 21, 22, 24, 25,32, 33, 38, 39, 40, 41, 50, 53, 57, 58,59, 60, 64	1, 2, 3,4, 5, 8, 9, 10, 11, 20, 25, 26, 30, 31, 42, 43, 44, 45, 46, 47, 48, 49, 54, 55, 62, 63

Answers with Rationales

1. After watching a movie of a train derailment, a child exclaims, "Wow, look how many cars fell off the tracks. There's junk everywhere. The engineer must have really been asleep." Using the facts that the child is impressed by the wreckage and assigns blame to the engineer, a follower of Piaget's theories would estimate the child to be about: (*Rigorous*)(*Skill 1.1*)

    A. ten years old
    B. twelve years old
    C. fourteen years old
    D. sixteen years old

The correct answer is A. According to Piaget's theory, children seven to eleven years old begin to apply logic to concrete things and experiences. They can combine performance and reasoning to solve problems. They have internalized moral values and are willing to confront rules and adult authority.

2. Children's literature became established in the: (*Rigorous*)(*Skill 1.1*)

    A. seventeenth century
    B. eighteenth century
    C. nineteenth century
    D. twentieth century

The correct answer is A. In the seventeenth century, Jean de la Fontaine's *Fables*, Pierre Perreault's *Tales*, Mme. d'Aulnoye's novels based on old folktales, and Mme. de Beaumont's *Beauty and the Beast* created a children's literature genre. In England, Perreault was translated, and a work allegedly written by Oliver Smith, *The Renowned History of Little Goody Two Shoes*, helped to establish children's literature in England, too.

3. **In the hierarchy of needs for adolescents who are becoming more team-oriented in their approach to learning, which need do they exhibit most?**
    (*Average Rigor*)(*Skill1.1*)

    A. Need for competence
    B. Need for love/acceptance
    C. Need to know
    D. Need to belong

The correct answer is B. Abraham's Maslow's theory of Humanistic Development states that such older children and adolescents exhibit most a need for love/acceptance from peers and potential romantic partners. Their need for competence is in the service of gaining the love/acceptance. Their need to know is developing, but is not their primary issue. Their need to belong does not address their emerging sexual identities.

4. **Which aspect of language is innate?**
    (*Rigorous*)(*Skill 2.1*)

    A. Biological capability to articulate sounds understood by other humans
    B. Cognitive ability to create syntactical structures
    C. Capacity for using semantics to convey meaning in a social environment
    D. Ability to vary inflections and accents

The correct answer is A. The biological capability to articulate sounds understood by other humans is innate, and later, children learn semantics and syntactical structures through trial and error. Linguists agree that language is first a vocal system of word symbols that enable a human to communicate his or her feelings, thoughts, and desires to other human beings.

5. **The most significant drawback to applying learning theory research to classroom practice is that:**
    (Rigorous)(Skill2.2)

    A. today's students do not acquire reading skills with the same alacrity as when greater emphasis was placed on reading classical literature
    B. development rates are complicated by geographical and cultural differences that are difficult to overcome
    C. homogeneous grouping has contributed to faster development of some age groups
    D. social and environmental conditions have contributed to an escalated maturity level than research done twenty or more years ago would seem to indicate

The correct answer is D. A mismatch exists between what interests today's students and the learning materials presented to them. Choice A is a significant problem only if the school insists on using classical literature exclusively. Choice B does describe a drawback, but students are more alike in their disengagement from anachronistic learning materials than they are different due to their culture and geographical location. Choice C describes a situation that is not widespread.

6. **Computer-assisted instruction (CAI) accommodates all of the following factors in reading instruction _except for:_**
    (Average Rigor)(Skill 2.5)

    A. free-form responses to comprehension questions
    B. increased motivation
    C. the addition of speech with computer-presented text
    D. the use of computers for word processing, and the integration of writing instruction with reading

The correct answer is A. C does not accommodate free-form responses to comprehension questions and relies heavily on drill-and-practice and multiple-choice formats. This is a limitation of CAI.

7. **To explain or to inform belongs in the category of** (*Average Rigor*)(*Skill 3.1*)

    A. exposition.
    B. narration.
    C. persuasion.
    D. description.

The answer is A. Exposition sets forth a systematic explanation of any subject and informs the audience about various topics. It can also introduce the characters of a story and their situations as the story begins. Narration tells a story. Persuasion seeks to influence an audience so that they will adopt some new point of view or take some action. Description provides sensory details and addresses spatial relationships of objects.

8. **Modeling is a practice that requires students to:** (*Rigorous*)(*Skill 3.1*)

    A. create a style unique to their own language capabilities
    B. emulate the writing of professionals
    C. paraphrase passages from good literature
    D. peer evaluate the writings of other students.

The correct answer is B. Modeling engages students in analyzing the writing of professional writers and in imitating the syntactical, grammatical, and stylistic mastery of that writer. Choice A is an issue of voice. Choice C is a less rigorous form of the correct answer. Choice D is only very indirectly related to modeling.

9. **Which level of meaning is the hardest aspect of a language to master?** (*Rigorous*)(*Skill 3.2*)

    A. denotation
    B. jargon
    C. connotation
    D. slang

The answer is C. Connotation refers to the meanings suggested by a word, rather than the dictionary definition. For example, the word 'slim' means thin, and it is usually used with a positive connotation, to compliment of admire someone's figure. The word 'skinny' also means thin, but its connotations are not as flattering as those of the word 'slim'. The connotative aspect of language is more difficult to master than the denotation (dictionary definition), as the former requires a mastery of the social aspect of language, not just the linguistic rules.

10. **Which of the following terms does *not* denote a figure of speech (figurative language)?** *(Rigorous)(Skill 3.2)*

   A. Simile
   B. Euphemism
   C. Onomatopoeia
   D. Allusion

The correct answer is D. An allusion is an implied reference to a famous person, event, thing, or a part of another text. A simile is a direct comparison between two things. A euphemism is the substitution of an agreeable or inoffensive term for one that might offend. Onomatopoeia is vocal imitation to convey meaning— "bark" or "meow"-- are examples.

11. **The appearance of a Yankee from Connecticut in the Court of King Arthur is an example of a/an:** *(Rigorous)(Skill3.2)*

   A. rhetoric
   B. parody
   C. paradox
   D. anachronism

The correct answer is D. Anachronism is the placing of characters, persons, events, or things into time frames incongruent with their actual dates. Parody is poking fun at something. Paradox is a seeming contradiction. Anachronism is something out of time frame.

12. **This statement, "I'll die if I don't pass this course," exemplifies a/an:** *(Average Rigor)(Skill 3.2)*

   A. barbarism
   B. oxymoron
   C. hyperbole
   D. antithesis

The correct answer is C. A hyperbole is an exaggeration for the sake of emphasis. It is a figure of speech not meant to be taken literally. A barbarism is the use of incorrect or unacceptable language. An oxymoron is a term comprised of opposite or incongruous elements, such as the term "peace fighter."

13. **A figure of speech in which someone absent or something inhuman is addressed as though present and able to respond describes:**
(Average Rigor)(Skill 3.2)

   A. personification
   B. synecdoche
   C. metonymy
   D. apostrophe

The correct answer is D. An apostrophe differs from a personification in the important respect that a "someone" cannot be "personified," plus personifications come in far more varieties than are suggested by the definition in question. A synecdoche is a figure of speech which represents some whole or group by one of its or their parts or members. Metonymy is the substitution of a word for a related word.

14. ***Diction* is best defined as:**
(Average Rigor)(Skill 3.2)

   A. the specific word choices an author makes in order to create a particular mood or feeling in the reader
   B. writing that explains something thoroughly
   C. the background, or exposition, for a short story or drama
   D. word choices that help teach a truth or moral

The correct answer is A. Diction refers to an author's choice of words, expressions, and style to convey his/her meaning. The other choices are only marginally related to this meaning, so the choice is a clear one.

15. **The literary device of personification is used in which example below? (Easy)(Skill3.2)**

   A. "Beg me no beggary by soul or parents, whining dog!"
   B. "Happiness sped through the halls cajoling as it went."
   C. "O wind thy horn, thou proud fellow."
   D. "And that one talent which is death to hide."

The correct answer is B. Personification is defined as giving human characteristics to inanimate objects or concepts. It can be thought of as a sub-category of metaphor. Happiness, an abstract concept, is "speeding through the halls" and "cajoling," both of which are human behaviors, so Happiness is being compared to a human being. Choice A is figurative and metaphorical but not a personification. Choice C is, again, figurative and metaphorical, but not a personification. The speaker is, perhaps, telling someone that they are bragging or "blowing their own horn." Choice D is also figurative and metaphorical but not personification. Hiding a particular talent is being compared to risking death.

16. **Read the following passage:**

   "It would have been hard to find a passer-by more wretched in appearance. He was a man of middle height, stout and hardy, in the strength of maturity; he might have been forty-six or seven. A slouched leather cap hid half his face, bronzed by the sun and wind, and dripping with sweat."

   What is its main form of discourse? (*Easy)(Skill3.2*)

   A. Description
   B. Narration
   C. Exposition
   D. Persuasion

The correct answer is A. The passage describes the appearance of a person in detail. Narration tells a story. Exposition explains or informs. Persuasion promotes a point of view or course of action.

17. **A paper written in first person and having characters, a setting, a plot, some dialogue, and events sequenced chronologically with some flashbacks exemplifies which genre?**(*Easy) (Skill 3.2)*

    A. Exposition
    B. Narration
    C. Persuasion
    D. Speculation

The correct answer is B. Narrative writing tells a story, and all the listed elements pertain to stories. Expository writing explains or informs. Persuasive writing states an opinion and attempts to persuade an audience to accept the opinion or to take some specified action. Speculative writing explores possible developments from given circumstances.

18. **"Clean as a whistle" and "easy as falling off a log" exemplify:** *(Easy)(Skill 3.2)*

    A. semantics
    B. parody
    C. irony
    D. clichés

The correct answer is D. A cliché is a phrase or expression that has become dull due to overuse. Semantics is a field of language study. Parody is poking fun at something. Irony is using language to create an unexpected or opposite meaning of the literal words being used.

19. **Middle school students bring little, if any, initial experience in** *(Rigorous)(Skill 3.3)*

    A. phonics
    B. phonemics
    C. textbook reading assignments
    D. stories read by the teacher

The correct answer is C. In middle school, probably for the first time, the student will be expected to read textbook assignments and come to class prepared to discuss the content. Students get phonics (the systematic study of decoding) in the early grades, and they normally get phonemics (familiarity with the syllable sounds of English) even earlier. They will have almost certainly had stories read to them by a teacher by the time they get to middle school.

20. **Regularly requiring students to practice reading short, instructional-level texts at least three times to a peer and to give and receive peer feedback about these readings mainly addresses which reading skill?**(*Average Rigor*)(*Skill 3.6*)

    A. Comprehension
    B. Fluency
    C. Evaluation
    D. Word-solving

The correct answer is B. Fluency is the ability to read text quickly with accuracy, phrasing, and expression. Fluency develops over time and requires substantial reading practice. This activity provides just this sort of practice. The peer feedback portion does address comprehension, evaluation, and some word-solving, but the main thrust is on fluency development.

21. **Before reading a passage, a teacher gives her students an anticipation guide with a list of statements related to the topic they are about to cover in the reading material. She asks the students to indicate their agreement or disagreement with each statement on the guide. This activity is intended to (*Average Rigor*) (*Skill 3.6*)**

    A. elicit students' prior knowledge of the topic and set a purpose for reading
    B. help students to identify the main ideas and supporting details in the text
    C. help students to synthesize information from the text
    D. help students to visualize the concepts and terms in the text

The correct answer is A. Establishing a purpose for reading, the foundation for a reading unit or activity, is intimately connected to activating the students' prior knowledge in strategic ways. When the reason for reading is developed in the context of the students' experiences, they are far better prepared to succeed because they can make connections from a base they thoroughly understand. This influences motivation, and with proper motivation, students are more enthused and put forward more effort to understand the text. The other choices are only indirectly supported by this activity and are more specific in focus.

22. **A conversation between two or more people is called a/an:** *(Easy)* *(Skill 4.3)*

   A. parody
   B. dialogue
   C. monologue
   D. analogy

The correct answer is B. Dialogues are the conversations virtually indispensable to dramatic work, and they often appear in narrative and poetry, as well. A parody is a work that adopts the subject and structure of another work in order to ridicule it. A monologue is a work or part of a work written in the first person. An analogy illustrates an idea by means of a more familiar one that is similar or parallel to it.

23. **Among junior-high school students of low-to-average readability levels, which work would most likely stir reading interest?** *(Average Rigor)(Skill4.3)*

   A. *Elmer Gantry*, Sinclair Lewis
   B. *Smiley's People*, John Le Carre
   C. *The Outsiders*, S.E. Hinton
   D. *And Then There Were None*, Agatha Christie.

The correct answer is C. The students can easily identify with the characters, the social issues, the vocabulary, and the themes in the book. The book deals with teenage concerns such as fitting-in, cliques, and appearance in ways that have proven very engaging for young readers.

24. Consider the following poem:

My name is John Welington Wells,
I'm a dealer in magic and spells,
In blessings and curses,
And ever-fill'd purses,
In prophecies, witches, and knells.

This poem would be considered a:
(Average Rigor)(Skill 4.3)

A. sonnet
B. haiku
C. limerick
D. cinquain

The correct answer is C. A limerick is a five line, humorous verse(often nonsensical) with a rhyme scheme of *aabba* . Lines 1, 2, and 5 usually have eight syllables each, and lines 3 and 4 have five syllables. Line 5 is often some type of "zinger." A sonnet is a 14-line poem in iambic pentameter and has a definite rhyme scheme. Shakespearean and Petrarchan sonnets are the main varieties. A cinquain is a five-line poem with one word in line 1, two words in line 2, and so on through line 5.

25. Which of the following would be the most significant factor in teaching Homer's *Iliad* and *Odyssey* to any particular group of students?*(Rigorous)(Skill4.3)*

A. Identifying a translation on the appropriate reading level
B. Determining the student's interest level
C. Selecting an appropriate evaluative technique
D. Determining the scope and delivery methods of background study

The correct answer is A. Students will appreciate these two works if the translation reflects both the vocabulary they know and their reading level. Choice B is moot because most students aren't initially interested in Homer. Choice C skips to later matters. Choice D is tempting and significant but not as crucial as having an accessible text.

26. **If a student uses slang and expletives, what is the best course of action to take in order to improve the student's formal communication skills?** *(Easy)(Skill 4.4)*

   A. Ask the student to rephrase their writing; that is, translate it into language appropriate for the school principal to read
   B. Refuse to read the student's papers until he conforms to a more literate style
   C. Ask the student to read his work aloud to the class for peer evaluation
   D. Rewrite the flagrant passages to show the student the right form of expression

The correct answer is A. Asking the student to write to the principal, a respected authority figure, will alert the student to the need to use formal language. Simply refusing to read the paper is not only negative, but it also sets up a power struggle. Asking the student to read slang and expletives aloud to the class for peer evaluation is to risk unproductive classroom chaos and to support the class clowns. Rewriting the flagrant passages for the student to model formal expression does not immerse the student in the writing process.

27. **Oral debate is most closely associated with which form of discourse?** *(Easy)(Skill 4.4)*

   A. Description
   B. Exposition
   C. Narration
   D. Persuasion

The correct answer is D. The purpose of a debate is to convince an audience or set of judges about something which is very much the same as persuading some audience or set of judges about something.

28. **The substitution of "went to his rest" for "died" exemplifies a/an:** *(Easy)(Skill 4.4)*

   A. bowdlerism
   B. jargon
   C. euphemism
   D. malapropism

The correct answer is C. A euphemism alludes to a distasteful topic in a pleasant manner in order to obscure or soften the disturbing impact of the original. A bowdlerism is a prudish version of something. Jargon is language specific to some occupation or activity. A malapropism is the improper use of a word that sounds like the word that would fit the context. The result is most often ludicrous.

29. The students in Mrs. Cline's seventh grade language arts class were invited to attend a performance of *Romeo and Juliet* presented by the drama class at the high school. To best prepare, they should: *(Rigorous) (Skill 4.4)*

   A. read the play as a homework exercise
   B. read a synopsis of the plot and a biographical sketch of the author
   C. examine a few main selections from the play to become familiar with the language and style of the author
   D. read a condensed version of the story and practice attentive listening skills

The correct answer is D. By reading a condensed version of the play, students will know the plot and therefore be better able to follow the play on stage. They will also practice being attentive. Choice A is far less dynamic and few will do it. Choice B is likewise dull. Choice C is not thorough enough.

30. Which of the following is the least effective procedure for promoting consciousness of audience? *(Rigorous)(Skill 4.7)*

   A. Pairing students during the writing process
   B. Reading all rough drafts before the students write the final copies
   C. Having students compose stories or articles for publication in school literary magazines or newspapers
   D. Writing letters to friends or relatives

The correct answer is B. Reading all rough drafts will do the least to promote consciousness of audience. Students are very used to turning papers into the teacher, and most don't think much about impressing the teacher. Pairing students will ensure a small, constant audience about whom they care, and having them compose stories for literary magazines will encourage them to put their best efforts forward because their work will be read by an actual audience in an impressive format. Writing letters also engages students in thinking about how best to communicate with a particular audience.

31. **A student informative composition should consist of a minimum of how many paragraphs?***(Average Rigor)(Skill 4.7)*

   A. Three
   B. Four
   C. Five
   D. Six

The correct answer is C. This composition would consist of an introductory paragraph, three body paragraphs, and a concluding paragraph. A three or four paragraph composition could include all three types of paragraphs but would not require the students to elaborate at sufficient length in the body of the paper. A six paragraph minimum is slightly excessive.

32. **In 'inverted triangle' introductory paragraphs, the thesis sentence occurs:**
   (Average Rigor)(Skill 4.7)

   A. at the beginning of the paragraph
   B. in the middle of the paragraph
   C. at the end of the paragraph
   D. in the second paragraph

The correct answer is C. The beginning of the paragraph should establish interest, the middle of the paragraph should establish a general context, and the paragraph should end with the thesis that the rest of the paper will develop. Delaying the thesis until the second paragraph would be "outside the triangle."

33. **A punctuation mark indicating omission, interrupted thought, or an incomplete statement is a/an:** *(Easy) (Skill 4.8)*

   A. ellipsis
   B. anachronism
   C. colloquy
   D. idiom

The correct answer is A. In an ellipsis, a word or words that would clarify the sentence's message are missing, yet it is still possible to understand them from the context. An anachronism is something out of its proper time frame. A colloquy is a formal conversation or dialogue. An idiom is a saying peculiar to some language group.

34. Which of the four underlined sections of the following sentence contains an error that a word processing spellchecker probably **wouldn't** catch? (Easy)(Skill 4.8)

He *tuc* the *hors* by the *rains* and pulled it back to the *stabel*.

A. tuc
B. hors
C. rains
D. stabel

The correct answer is C. Spellcheckers only catch errors in conventional modern English spelling. They cannot catch errors involving incorrect homophone usage. "Rains" is the only one of the four words to conform to conventional English spelling, but it clearly is not the word called for by the context.

35. For students with poor vocabularies, the teacher should recommend first that: *(Easy) (Skill 4.8)*

A. they enroll in a Latin class
B. they read newspapers, magazines, and books on a regular basis
C. they write the words repetitively after looking them up in the dictionary
D. they use a thesaurus to locate and incorporate the synonyms found there into their vocabularies

The correct answer is B. Regularly reading a wide variety of materials for pleasure and information is the best way to develop a stronger vocabulary. The other suggestions have limited application and do not serve to reinforce an enthusiasm for reading.

36. Which group of words is not a sentence? *(Easy)(Skill 4.8)*

A. In keeping with the graduation tradition, the students, in spite of the rain, standing in the cafeteria tossing their mortarboards.
B. Rosa Parks, who refused to give up her seat on the bus, will be forever remembered for her courage.
C. Taking advantage of the goalie's being out of the net, we scored our last and winning goal.
D. When it began to rain, we gathered our possessions and ran for the pavilion.

The correct answer is A. This is a sentence fragment because sentences require a subject and a verb and there is no verb. Changing "the students, in spite of the rain, standing" to "the students, in spite of the rain, were standing" corrects the problem.

37. The arrangement and relationship of words in sentences or sentence structures best describes: *(Average Rigor) (Skill 4.8)*

A. style
B. discourse
C. thesis
D. syntax

The correct answer is D. Syntax is the grammatical structure of sentences. Style is not limited to considerations of syntax only, but it includes vocabulary, voice, genre, and other language features. Discourse refers to investigating some idea. A thesis is a statement of opinion.

38. Identify the sentence that has an error in parallel structure. *(Average Rigor)(Skill 4.8)*

A. In order to help your favorite cause, you should contribute time or money, raise awareness, and write congressmen.
B. Many people envision scientists working alone in a laboratory and discovering scientific breakthroughs.
C. Some students prefer watching videos to textbooks because they are used for visual presentation.
D. Tom Hanks, who has won two Academy Awards, is celebrated as an actor, director, and producer.

The correct answer is C. Parallel structure means that certain sentence structures in key positions match up grammatically. In choice C, "watching videos" is a gerund phrase functioning as the direct object of the verb, and, because the verb implies a comparison, parallel construction requires that "textbooks" (functioning as the object of a currently missing gerund) be preceded by an appropriate gerund--in this case, "reading." In order for the structure to be parallel, the sentence should read "Some students prefer <u>watching videos</u> to <u>*reading* textbooks</u> because they are used for visual presentation." They prefer something to something else. The other sentences conform to parallel structure. Recognizing parallel structure requires a sophisticated understanding of grammar.

39. **Consider the following sentence:**

   Joe <u>didn't hardly know his cousin Fred</u>, who'd had a rhinoplasty.
   Which word group below best conveys the intended meaning of the underlined section above? *(Average Rigor)(Skill 4.8)*

   A. hardly did know his cousin Fred
   B. didn't know his cousin Fred hardly
   C. hardly knew his cousin Fred
   D. didn't know his cousin Fred

The correct answer is C. It contains a correctly-phrased negative expressed in the appropriate tense. Choice A has tense and awkwardness problems. Choice B has tense and double negative problems. Choice D ignores the fact that he knew Fred a little.

40. **Which of the following bits of information best describes the structure of English?** *(Average Rigor)(Skill 4.8)*

   A. Syntax based on word order
   B. Inflected
   C. Romantic
   D. Orthography is phonetic

The correct answer is A. The syntax of English, reflective of its Germanic origins, relies on word order rather than inflection. Because of this and the many influences of other languages (particularly with regard to vocabulary), the orthography is not phonetic which complicates the teaching of standardized spelling.

41. Use the table below to answer the question that follows it.

	Math Usage	General Usage
bi (two)	bilinear	bicycle
	bimodal	biplane
	binomial	bifocals
cent (100)	centimeter	century
	centigram	centigrade
	percent	centipede
circum (around)	circumference	circumnavigate
	circumradius	circumstance
	circumcenter	Circumspect

Which vocabulary strategy does the table above exemplify?
(Rigorous)(Skill4.8)

A. Frayer method
B. Morphemic analysis
C. Semantic mapping
D. Word mapping

The correct answer is B. Morphemes are the smallest units of language that have an associated meaning. The purpose of morphemic analysis is to apply morphemic awareness to the task of learning new words. The Frayer method involves having students use their own words to define new words and to link those definitions to personal experiences. Semantic mapping incorporates graphical clues to concepts and is a subset of graphic organizers. Word mapping is another subset of graphic organizers and consists of displaying such information as the various forms a word may take as it transforms through the parts of speech.

42. **Which of the following contains an error in possessive punctuation?**
(Rigorous)(Skill 4.8)

A. Doris's shawl
B. mother's-in-law frown
C. children's lunches
D. ambassador's briefcase

The correct answer is B. Mother-in-law is a compound, common noun, and the apostrophe should come at the end of the word according to convention. The other choices are correctly punctuated.

43. Which of the following sentences is unambiguously properly punctuated? (*Rigorous)(Skill 4.8*)

A. The more you eat; the more you want.
B. The authors—John Steinbeck, Ernest Hemingway, and William Faulkner—are staples of modern writing in American literature textbooks.
C. Handling a wild horse, takes a great deal of skill and patience
D. The man, who replaced our teacher, is a comedian.

The correct answer is B. Dashes should be used instead of commas when commas are used elsewhere in the sentence for amplification or explanation as seen here within the dashes. Choice A has a semicolon where there should be a comma. Choice C has a comma that shouldn't be there at all. Choice D could be correct in a non-restrictive context, and so whether or not it is correct is ambiguous.

44. Consider the following sentence:

Mr. Brown is a school volunteer <u>with a reputation and twenty years service</u>.

Which phrase below best represents the logical intent of the underlined phrase above? (*Rigorous)(Skill 4.8*)

A. with a reputation for twenty years' service
B. with a reputation for twenty year's service
C. who has served twenty years
D. with a service reputation of twenty years

The correct answer is D. His reputation pertains to his service performance, not its duration. Choice A implies that it was for its duration. Choice B has Choice A's problem plus an incorrectly punctuated possessive. Choice C ignores his service reputation.

45. Which of the following sentences contains an error in agreement? (*Rigorous)(Skill 4.8*)

A. Jennifer is one of the women who writes for the magazine.
B. Each one of their sons plays a different sport.
C. This band has performed at the Odeum many times.
D. The data are available online at the listed website.

The correct answer is A. "Women" is the plural antecedent of the relative pronoun "who," which is functioning as the subject in its clause; so "who" is plural and requires the 3rd person plural form for the verb "write."

46. **Which item below is not a research-based strategy that supports reading?** *(Rigorous)(Skill 4.9)*

   A. Reading more
   B. Reading along with a more proficient reader
   C. Reading a passage no more than twice
   D. Self-monitoring progress

The correct answer is C. Actually, research shows that reading a passage several times improves fluency, and, depending on the complexity of the material, improves comprehension, too. The more complex the material, the more comprehension value comes from repeated readings.

47. **All of the following techniques are used to conduct ongoing informal assessment of student progress _except for:_** *(Rigorous) (Skill 5.1)*

   A. analyzing the student work product at key stages
   B. collecting data from assessment tests
   C. posing strategic questions
   D. observing students as they work

The correct answer is B. The key here hinges on the adjective "informal." Assessment tests employ standardized materials and formats to monitor student progress and to report it in statistical terms. The other choices are relatively informal, teacher-specific techniques addressing more current, lesson-specific products and dynamics.

48. **A formative evaluation of student writing:** *(Rigorous) (Skill 5.1)*

   A. requires a thorough marking of mechanical errors with a pencil or pen
   B. makes comments on the appropriateness of the student's interpretation of the prompt and the degree to which the objective was met
   C. requires the student to hand in all the materials produced during the process of writing
   D. involves several careful readings of the text for content, mechanics, spelling, and usage

The correct answer is B. Formative evaluations should support the students' writing process through strategic feedback at key points. Teacher comments and feedback should encourage recursive revision and metacognition. Choice A applies, if anywhere, to a summative evaluation of student writing. Choice C is a neutral management strategy. A teacher can make formative evaluations without collecting all the materials. Choice D, again, is more suited for summative evaluation or for the very last issue in the composition process, namely proofreading.

49. Effective assessment requires that: *(Average Rigor) (Skill 5.1)*

    A. students not be involved in the assessment process
    B. testing activities are kept separate from the teaching activities
    C. references materials that classroom instruction has prepared the students to read
    D. tests, in order to be reliable, should never use materials previously studied in the classroom

The correct answer is C. The only reliable measure of the success of a unit will be based on the reading on which the instruction has focused. Choice A makes almost no sense; students will at the very least have to do something that can be assessed. Choice B calls into question the whole reason for schools. Choice D uses different phrases to accomplish the same unworthy end as choice B.

50. Effective assessment means that: *(Easy) (Skill 5.2)*

    A. it ignores age and cultural considerations
    B. students' weaknesses are emphasized
    C. only reading skills count
    D. it is integrated with instruction and is not intrusive

The correct answer is D. Effective assessment informs instruction and practice. It is one phase of an integrated instructional cycle. Choice A ignores reality and distorts rather than informs. Choice B discourages students. Choice C ignores other important ways of demonstrating growth in understanding.

51. A paper explaining the relationship between food and weight gain contains the signal words "because," "consequently," "this is how," and "due to." These words suggest that the paper has which text structure? *(Easy)(Skill 5.2)*

    A. Cause and effect structure
    B. Compare and contrast structure
    C. Descriptive structure
    D. Sequential structure

The correct answer is A. These signal words connect events in a causal chain, creating an explanation of some process or event. Compare and contrast structure presents similarities and differences. Descriptive structure presents a sensory impression of something or someone. Sequential structure references what comes first, next, last, and so on.

TEACHER CERTIFICATION EXAM

52. **To enhance reading comprehension, experts recommend all of these techniques _except for_: (Average Rigor) (Skill 5.2)**

    A. reading material through only once, but read slowly and carefully
    B. reading material through more than once according to a plan
    C. creating a map for the next reading
    D. highlighting or taking notes during reading

The correct answer is A. While reading at a rate that assures accuracy is desirable, there is no evidence to support a recommendation to avoid rereading something. Choice B is advisable because it proposes a purpose for the rereadings. Choice C is advisable because it also addresses purpose. Choice D is advisable because it helps students maintain focus as they read.

53. **A composition with no voice will lack the following quality _(Rigorous)_ (Skill 5.2)**

    A. organization
    B. appeal
    C. illustrations
    D. ideas

The answer is B. Voice in writing refers to an author's tone, point of view or manner of communicating. A composition may have good ideas, organization and illustrations or example, but without voice, it will lack character and will not be appealing reading.

54. **Varying the complexity of a graphic organizer exemplifies differentiating which aspect of a lesson? _(Rigorous)(Skill 5.2)_**

    A. Its content/topic
    B. Its environment
    C. Its process
    D. Its product

The correct answer is C. Differentiating the process means offering a variety of learning activities or strategies to students as they manipulate the ideas embedded within the lesson concept. For example, students may use graphic organizers, maps, diagrams, or charts to display their comprehension of concepts covered. Varying the complexity of a graphic organizer can very effectively accommodate differing levels of cognitive processing so that students of differing ability are appropriately engaged. Lesson topic and content remain the same, the lesson is still taking place in the same environment, and in most lessons, the graphic organizer is not the product of the lesson.

MIDDLE GRADES ENG. 5-9   128

55. **A teacher has taught his students to self-monitor their reading by locating where in the passage they are having difficulty, by identifying the specific problem there, and by restating the difficult sentence or passage in their own words. These strategies are examples of: (Rigorous) (Skill 5.2)**

   A. graphic and semantic organizers
   B. metacognition
   C. recognizing story structure
   D. summarizing

The correct answer is C. Good readers use metacognitive strategies (various ways of thinking about thinking) to improve their reading. Before reading, they clarify their purpose for reading and preview the text. During reading, they monitor their understanding, adjusting their reading speed to fit the difficulty of the text and fixing any comprehension problems they have. After reading, they check their understanding of what they read.

56. **Reading assessment should take place: (Average Rigor) (Skill 5.3)**

   A. at the end of the semester
   B. at the end of a unit
   C. constantly
   D. all of the above

The correct answer is D. End-of-unit and end-of-semester measurements yield important information regarding achievement of course objectives and the evaluating of students' growth; however, assessment should be ongoing so that the teacher can adjust instruction to meet the day-to-day needs of the students.

57. Overcrowded classes prevent the individual attention needed to facilitate language development. This drawback can be best overcome by *(Average Rigor) (Skill 5.3)*

    A. dividing the class into independent study groups
    B. assigning more study time at home
    C. using more drill practice in class
    D. team teaching

The correct answer is A. Dividing a class into small groups maximizes opportunities for engagement. Assigning more study time at home is passing the responsibility onto the parents/caregivers. Using more drill practice in class is likely to bore most students to tears. Team teaching begs the question; if you can get another teacher, then your class should no longer be overcrowded.

58. Which of the following is not true about English? *(Easy)(Skill 5.3)*

    A. English is the easiest language to learn
    B. English is the least inflected language
    C. English has the most extensive vocabulary of any language
    D. English originated as a Germanic tongue

The correct answer is A. English has its own inherent quirks which make it difficult to learn, plus it has incorporated words, and even structures, from many disparate language groups in its lexicon and syntax. Languages with lexicons limited to words governed by a consistent set of relatively simple rules exist, so English is certainly not the easiest language to learn.

59. **Which of the following responses to literature typically give middle school students the most problems?** *(Rigorous)(Skill 6.1)*

    A. Interpretive
    B. Evaluative
    C. Critical
    D. Emotional

The correct answer is B. Middle school readers will exhibit both emotional and interpretive responses. In middle/junior high school, organized study models enable students to identify main ideas and supporting details, to recognize sequential order, to distinguish fact from opinion, and to determine cause/effect relationships. Middle school students can provide reasons to support their assertions that a particular book was boring or a particular poem made him or her feel sad, and this is to provide a critical reaction on a fundamental level. Evaluative responses, however, require students to address how the piece represents its genre, how well it reflects the social and ethical mores of a given society, or how well the author has employed a fresh approach to the subject. Evaluative responses are more sophisticated than critical responses, and they are most appropriate for advanced high school students.

60. **Writing ideas quickly without interruption of the flow of thoughts or attention to conventions is called:** *(Average Rigor) (Skill 6.2)*

    A. brainstorming
    B. mapping
    C. listing
    D. free writing

The correct answer is D. Free writing is a particular type of brainstorming (techniques used to generate ideas). Mapping is another type of brainstorming which results in products resembling flow charts. Listing is another brainstorming technique that differs from free writing in that free writing is more open-ended and looks more like sentences.

61. **In a timed essay test of an hour's duration, how much time should be devoted to prewriting?** *(Rigorous)(Skill 6.2)*

    A. Five minutes
    B. Ten minutes
    C. Fifteen minutes
    D. Twenty minutes

The correct answer is B. Ten minutes of careful planning allows sufficient time for the other stages of the writing process. Five minutes would result in dead-ends and backtracking during the writing. Fifteen and twenty minutes would result in rushing during the drafting, revising, and editing stages.

62. **Which of the following is not a technique of prewriting?** *(Average Rigor)(Skill 6.2)*

    A. Clustering
    B. Listing
    C. Brainstorming
    D. Proofreading

The answer is D. You cannot proofread something that you have not yet written. While it is true that prewriting involves written techniques, prewriting is not concerned with punctuation, capitalization, and spelling (proofreading). Brainstorming is a general term denoting generating ideas, and clustering and listing are specific methods of brainstorming.

63. **Reading a piece of student writing to assess the overall impression of the product is** *(Average Rigor) (Skill 6.2)*

   A. holistic evaluation.
   B. portfolio assessment.
   C. analytical evaluation.
   D. using a performance system.

The answer is A. In holistic scoring, the teacher reads quickly through a paper once to get a general impression and assigns a rating based on a rubric that includes the criteria for achievement in a few, key dimensions of the assignment. Portfolio assessment involves tracking work over stages or over time. Analytical evaluation involves breaking down the assignment into discrete traits and determining achievement in each of those traits. A performance system refers to engaging students in writing assignments meant to generate products in a given time frame. Often, such products are scored holistically.

64. **Which of the following should not be included in the opening paragraph of an informative essay?** *(Average Rigor)(Skill 6.3)*

   A. Thesis sentence
   B. Details and examples supporting the main idea
   C. Broad general introduction to the topic
   D. A style and tone that grabs the reader's attention

The correct answer is B. The introductory paragraph should introduce the topic, capture the reader's interest, state the thesis, and prepare the reader for the main points in the essay. Details and examples, however, belong in the second part of the essay, the body paragraphs.

9 781642 390100